ROBERT FRANCIS KENNEDY

November 20, 1925–June 6, 1968

My brother need not be idealized or enlarged in death beyond what he was in life. He should be remembered simply as a good and decent man who saw wrong and tried to right it, saw suffering and tried to heal it, saw war and tried to stop it.

Those of us who loved him and who take him to his rest today pray that what he was to us, and what he wished for others, will someday come to pass for all the world.

As he said many times, in many parts of this nation, to those he touched and who sought to touch him:

"Some men see things as they are and say why. I dream things that never were and say, why not."

—EDWARD M. KENNEDY

From the eulogy delivered at the funeral of his brother, Senator Robert F. Kennedy, at St. Patrick's Cathedral, New York, June 8, 1968

RFK

HIS LIFE AND DEATH

E 70 1

BY THE EDITORS OF
AMERICAN HERITAGE
The Magazine of History

Narrative by
Jay Jacobs

With an eyewitness account of The Last Thirty-six Hours by
Kristi N. Witker

A DELL BOOK

Staff

Editor: Alvin M. Josephy Jr.

Managing Editor: Kenneth W. Leish

Narrative: **Jay Jacobs**

Additional Text: Kristi N. Witker

Art Directors: Irwin M. Glusker, Richard Glassman

Picture Researchers: Wesley Day, Carla Davidson

Copy Editors: Brenda Bennerup, Helen C. Dunn

Text Researchers: Susan D. Eikov, Ellen C. Ehrlich, Michael Harwood, Nancy Kelly, Annette Welles

Editorial Assistants: Peggy Buckwalter, Mildred Ritter, Muriel Vrotsos

Published by Dell Publishing Co., Inc.
750 Third Avenue, New York, N.Y. 10017
Copyright © 1968 by American Heritage Publishing Co., Inc.
Library of Congress Catalog Card Number: 68–8987.
Dell ® TM 681510 Dell Publishing Co., Inc.
First Dell Printing June, 1968   Printed in U.S.A.

TABLE OF CONTENTS

Aeschylus wrote: "In our sleep, pain that cannot forget falls drop by drop upon the heart and in our own despair, against our will, comes wisdom through the awful grace of God."

What we need in the United States . . . is love and wisdom and compassion toward one another, and a feeling of justice toward those who still suffer within our own country, whether they be white or they be black.

Let us dedicate ourselves to what the Greeks wrote so many years ago: to tame the savageness of man and make gentle the life of the world. Let us dedicate ourselves to that, and say a prayer for our country and for our people.

—ROBERT F. KENNEDY

Extemporaneous remarks on the death of Martin Luther King, Jr., Indianapolis, Indiana, April 4, 1968

PROLOGUE

As dawn made its slow westward sweep across the North American continent that Tuesday, the Pop artist Andy Warhol lay fighting for his life in New York's Columbus Hospital after having been struck by three bullets the previous afternoon. In Boston, Dr. Benjamin Spock and four codefendants rose early and readied themselves for still another wearying day in court, where they were being tried for advocating resistance to the draft. In Tampa and its environs, storm-battered Floridians peered out across the waters of the Gulf of Mexico, hoping they had seen the last of Hurricane Abby despite predictions of her return. As the sun rose higher over the Eastern Seaboard, officials at Columbia University, edgy after weeks of campus rioting, nervously awaited the afternoon's commencement exercises, while in rural South Dakota, early rising farmers downed quick breakfasts and prepared to drive to the polling places. A little later on, California voters would be stirring, for it was their primary day, too. Back in New York, the morning sunlight slanted down into Madison Avenue and onto a huge banner that proclaimed: R.F.K. IS ALIVE AND WELL IN L.A. And three thousand miles away, Don Drysdale, the Dodger pitcher who was scheduled to go after an unprecedented sixth straight shut out that night, slept. So did the presidential candidates and their entourages. On this one morning there was no reason for rising early; there was nothing they could do but wait. One of those candidates slept in a friend's house at Malibu.

Rising for most men means the abandonment of dreams; for the candidate, when he arose, the opposite would be the case; wakefulness would bring with it the continuance of a dream begun a generation earlier; a dream that had been realized once, only to be shattered by a terrible awakening—and that now was being dreamed again. Dawn broke gray and smoggy over Southern California. The candidate slept through it. The sun, obscured, rose higher. To the east, in South Dakota, the voting had begun.

The campaign thus far had been grueling. After a couple of triumphs in Indiana and Nebraska, things had suddenly gone wrong in Oregon, and now, as the candidate arose in the bedroom at Malibu, he knew that, politically, there might for him be no tomorrow. Still, there was nothing to do

10

The California campaign

but wait until evening, when the polls closed and the vote tallying began. He gathered several of his children, and shortly after noon, set off for the beach. The afternoon was cold, raw, and misty, and the sun failed to appear. The candidate doffed a gaudy sun shirt and dived into the rollers. At one point a couple of his kids began to flounder in the heavy surf and he had to dive for them. He emerged with a bruised forehead. It was the second minor head injury he had suffered in a little more than a week; a few days earlier, someone had thrown a rock from the midst of a crowd.

In Los Angeles, members of the candidate's entourage also arose late and milled aimlessly around the Ambassador Hotel. For them, too, there was nothing to do but wait. In the hotel's Embassy Room, television crews were setting up their equipment while campaign workers festooned the walls with banners and posters. It would be here, sometime during the night, that victory would be acknowledged or defeat conceded. An almost palpable gloom hung in the air; partly because of the weather; partly because of the natural anxiety of the moment (the candidate had announced a few days earlier that a loss here, in the nation's most populous state, would put an end to his run); partly because of physical and emotional exhaustion; and partly as a result of a series of small but disheartening mishaps that had marred the last few days of the campaign and had left everyone just a bit edgy: the rock-throwing incident; an exploding balloon that had suddenly revealed a constant but unspoken

dread; a similar incident in San Francisco's China-town, when a string of popping firecrackers had sent a shudder through the candidate's body; some damned fool in Long Beach taunting him about a family tragedy; the incident of the day before, when he had suddenly slumped to his knees while ad-dressing a rally in San Diego, and then had vomited in a john. The press corps hung around, trying, in the absence of the candidate, to spin stories out of thin air.

Meanwhile at Malibu, the candidate had aban-doned the beach, with its heavy surf rolling under leaden skies, and returned to his temporary quar-ters, where, despite his hollow-eyed exhaustion, he managed to work up enough enthusiasm to rough-house with his children. His wife, normally ebulli-ent, seemed strangely subdued as she watched the high-jinks in the swimming pool. Later in the after-noon, the gloom of the day settled in more heavily. Somehow, even the news that an early poll of Cali-fornians who had already voted showed him lead-ing his opponent by a respectable margin failed to cheer him. Finally, succumbing to the enthusiasm of a couple of close aides, he relaxed a bit and left for Los Angeles and a nap . . .

He awoke refreshed and eager; there is nothing like the end of an election day for getting a politi-cian's adrenalin into full flow. South Dakota was already won, and the California polls had closed. (In Dodger Stadium, Drysdale was mowing down the Pirates with cold efficiency.) The candidate prowled restlessly around the "royal suite" as the

returns began coming in. Nothing decisive had come through yet, but now defeat was unthinkable. He began to plot out his victory speech. The count from the Los Angeles area was agonizingly slow, but a few minutes before midnight his California campaign manager assured him that he had won, and went downstairs to whip up enthusiasm in the Embassy ballroom. A few moments later, the candidate and his wife made their way downstairs and ascended the podium. The room was packed and the heat stifling. Grinning broadly, the candidate faced the jubilant throng. He thanked his many aides: the mountainous Los Angeles football star "who said he'd take care of anyone who didn't vote for me," and the former Olympic decathlon champion who had campaigned with him; his brother-in-law, "who is ruthless but effective"; his dog; his wife—and on and on. The tiredness had fallen away, and he was obviously savoring the taste of victory. Finally, after a good-humored dig at the mayor of Los Angeles, an old opponent, it was over. The crowd pressed forward as he started to leave the platform. He hesitated briefly, then changed course and made for a back passageway.

Chapter 1

THE SEEDS OF DYNASTY

. . . The Irish say your trouble is their
trouble and your
   joy their joy? I wish
I could believe it;
I am troubled, I'm dissatisfied, I'm Irish.
              — MARIANNE MOORE

It was the time of the Great Hunger, when the potatoes shriveled and went black, a million peasants died, and those who could emigrated, penniless and possessing only what they wore, to America. County Wexford was not hit as hard as the rest of Ireland, but the rack-rent landlords, their incomes lost in the blighted counties, squeezed down hard on their tenant farmers. The rents skyrocketed, and life—tough enough in the best of times—became intolerable.

Patrick Kennedy was twenty-five in 1848, and was faced with a bleak future indeed. The youngest of three sons living in a cramped cottage under a thatched roof, he turned, as did a million like him, to the promise of America. In October of that year, with a priest's blessing and little else but the twenty dollars or so required for his passage, he hiked six miles along the Barrow River to the seaport of New Ross and boarded a crowded, stinking "coffin ship" bound for Noddle's Island in East Boston.

The trip itself was a fearful gamble, with the odds only 2 to 1 for survival. The air on board was as rancid as the meager supply of food; water was rank; the diseased, sardined below decks together with the healthy, spread fever like wildfire; tempers flared, and men murdered one another with impunity in the resultant brawls. For those who survived, illiterate and unskilled, there was only the hope of backbreaking labor. Patrick Kennedy was luckier than most and found work not as a hod carrier or ditchdigger, but as a cooper.

Like many another Irishman in East Boston, "Paddy" Kennedy must have wondered at times at the wisdom of his decision. Bad as things had been in County Wexford, they were in some ways worse in the Promised Land. At least the air had been soft and sweet in the old country, and the land— blighted praties notwithstanding—had been green. Irish Boston, on the other hand, was altogether unfit for human habitation; the cost of living (especially for a people unused to buying their food, and paid a dollar a day for working themselves into a stupor of exhaustion) was incredibly high; smallpox, typhus, and a host of other diseases were rife in the Noddle's Island ghetto. Bilked by conniving predators and detested by the WASP Establishment, Kennedy and his like must have looked back almost wistfully at times to the simple hard-fistedness of

ERECTED BY
PATRICK KENNEDY
DUNGANSTOWN IN MEMORY OF
HIS FATHER JAMES KENNEDY
WHO DIED 17TH FEB. 1881.
AGED 86 YEARS.
ALSO HIS MOTHER
CATHERINE KENNEDY, WHO DIED
18TH NOV. 1914, AGED 85 YEARS.
THE ABOVE PATRICK KENNEDY,
HIS 3 CHILDREN WHO DIED YOUNG.
ALSO HIS *JOHANNA KENNEDY*

ERECTED BY
JOHN KENNEDY
IN MEMORY OF HIS MOTHER
MARY KENNEDY (ALIAS GUNNIP)
OF *DUNGANSTOWN*
WHO DIED 30TH DEC. 1898, AGED 85 YRS.
ALSO HIS FATHER JOHN KENNEDY
WHO DIED 24TH MARCH 1864.
AGED 55 YEARS.
HIS SISTER CATHERINE WHO DIED
3RD MARCH 1908. AGED 55 YEARS.
ALSO THE ABOVE JOHN KENNEDY,
DIED 28TH MAR. 1924, AGED 67 YEARS.
AND HIS BROTHER PATRICK KENNEDY,
DIED 7TH JUNE 1927, AGED 84 YEARS.
ALSO HIS SISTER JOHANNA KENNEDY
DIED 27TH MARCH 1937, AGED 86
AND HIS BROTHER JAMES KENNEDY
DIED 7TH APRIL 1939, AGED 80

Tombstones in Dunganstown churchyard in Ireland mark graves of Robert F. Kennedy's paternal ancestors.

the landlords and the brutally repressive policies of the English in Ireland; the English, at least, had been *hereditary* enemies.

In such conditions, Patrick Kennedy married, sired three daughters and a son. Then in 1858, poor as the day he left Ireland and physically worn out, he died of cholera at thirty-five. He had lived just long enough to continue the Kennedy line—and, in the depths of abject poverty, to sow the seeds of a dynasty.

The beginnings of a dynasty are not always easily recognizable as such; there is no telling, for example, how many royal lines might trace their origins to some rude oaf who happened to swing a bludgeon a little faster than his neighbor, thereby acquiring a bit of real estate that eventually became a kingdom. In any event, there was little reason for his contemporaries to suspect that Patrick Joseph, the first male Kennedy born on these shores, was only two generations from the nearest thing to a royal family that this country has produced. P. J. left grammar school in his early teens and took a job as an East Boston dock-walloper to supplement the meager income his widowed mother eked out as a hairdresser. Physically, he was well suited to the job, but temperamentally, it seems, he had little inclination to follow in his father's footsteps to an early grave. P. J. labored only as long as he had to, saved every penny he could, and then set himself up in business as a saloonkeeper in Haymarket Square. By living frugally, reinvesting his profits, abstaining from his own stock, and taking advantage of his

Patrick J. Kennedy, the first member
of the family born in America, became a powerful politician and was
able to send his son Joe to Harvard.

opportunities, P. J. slowly but steadily made a success of his life. In due course he built up a thriving whiskey distributorship, bought his way into two more saloons (one of them, in the Maverick House, quite a posh establishment as East Boston watering places went in those days), and eventually drifted into Democratic politics. After serving in the Massachusetts House and then in the state Senate, he decided that the real power lay not in elective office, but in the potent, if ill-defined, role of ward boss. As a member of the Irish-dominated "Board of Strategy," Kennedy dispensed patronage, got out the vote, generally acted as a power behind the various political thrones, and numbered among his confreres one John F. Fitzgerald, of whom we shall hear more later. P. J. had married Mary Hickey, the daughter of a "lace-curtain" Irish family, in 1887. A year later their first son, Joseph Patrick, was born.

Although he had gone into politics, P. J. had not given up his business interests. On the contrary, he went after increasingly bigger game and eventually found himself involved in coal, banking, real estate, and the stock market. As a result of all this, young Joe Kennedy spent his formative years in cultivating a healthy appreciation for the not altogether unpleasant uses of money—and for the sort of industry and application through which money is attained. And, as a steady parade of local ward heelers appeared in the Kennedy parlor to pay tribute to his father (who, like most bosses of the day, saw to it that his constituents voted early and often), he also gained a healthy respect for the uses of power.

For all his political activity, Patrick J. Kennedy was not the stereotype of the gregarious Irishman. Introspective and somewhat austere, cut from soberer cloth than most of the Democratic politicos of his day, he stayed home when he could, read American history, and instructed his son (more by example than by precept) in the ways of the world. Family solidarity came naturally, almost inevitably, to the Kennedys. Better off than the vast majority of Boston Irish, but still scorned by the old Yankee Protestants, and somewhat scornful of most of their few Irish financial equals, they were more or less forced by circumstances into family insularity—a trait that was to become even more pronounced in the succeeding generation.

Possibly to impress his father—and certainly not out of need—young Joe engaged in a variety of money-making ventures during his childhood and teens. Like most of his coevals, he ran errands, hawked newspapers, and did odd jobs around the East Boston shops. Unlike most of them, though, he had a number of more enterprising schemes up his sleeve, including one whereby the pigeons of Boston Common were lured to an East Boston coop by a couple of homers, there to be converted into roast squabs, a delicacy much admired by gourmets in the Irish community. Even as a teen-age first baseman, Joe saw no reason for not mixing a little business with pleasure and soon convinced his sand-lot playmates of the logic of giving up their amateur standing. He rented a ball park on Locust Street for his team, the Assumptions, and made a fairly lucrative thing of selling tickets to their baseball games.

If Patrick J. Kennedy had learned one lesson from life in Boston it was that industry, thrift, and acumen might confer a measure of success—and even power—on an Irish Catholic, but that social acceptance, acceptance in the more rarified precincts of Yankee Protestantism, required something more. Determined that his offspring would one day walk through doors closed to himself, he discontinued young Joe's Catholic education and had him enrolled in Boston Latin School, an institution with a list of alumni that read like a New England Almanach de Gotha. As a scholar, Joe Kennedy excelled at extracurricular activities: he was colonel of the school's championship cadet drill regiment, president of the senior class (a senior class that left school a year before he did, thanks to his academic disinclinations), managed the football team, and played varsity basketball and baseball. As a ballplayer, Joe was later remembered as a spectacular (.667) hitter and a spectacularly sore loser who gave the umpires as hard a time as he gave the opposing pitchers. The editors of the 1908 school yearbook, prescient beyond their years, foresaw that his fortune would be made "in a very roundabout way." In defiance of both Yankee and Irish Catholic tradition, Joe Kennedy was enrolled at Harvard upon his belated graduation from Boston Latin. What he accomplished at Harvard (and it was little enough) did not matter. What mattered was simply that he *went*. As his biographer Richard J. Whalen put it, "Though still a trespasser in unyielding Yankee

Bobby's maternal grandparents, the John F. Fitzgeralds, on their fortieth wedding anniversary, in 1929

Boston, Kennedy could no longer be dismissed as a stranger."

Banking was the natural profession of a Bostonian and Harvard man in those days, but an Irish banker was an even greater anomaly than an Irish Harvard man (P. J. Kennedy was, of course, an exception, but he had *bought* his banking interests), and the little entree provided by his Harvard diploma was not enough to open the way to a banking career for young Joe Kennedy. ("A couple of the tellers are Irish," one banker is supposed to have assured John F. Fitzgerald, when the then mayor asked why there were no Irishmen on his board of directors—to which Fitzgerald is supposed to have replied: "Yes, and I suppose the charwomen are, too.") By pulling a few strings, though, the would-be financier was able to become a state bank examiner—a lowly white-collar job, but one that was to prove immensely profitable in the years to come. Joe held the job about a year and a half, during which time he thoroughly familiarized himself with the structure, strengths, and weaknesses of innumerable Massachusetts banking institutions. Then, in late 1913, P. J. enlisted his son's aid in what appeared to be a foredoomed attempt to save the Columbia Trust Company, a small bank in which he had an interest, from being swallowed up by a more solvent operation. After some desperate wheeling and dealing, Joe Kennedy—not much more than a year out of college—not only saved Columbia Trust but got himself elected to its presidency.

A couple of years earlier, P. J.'s old political

Joseph P. Kennedy and Rose Fitzgerald were married in October, 1914, by Boston's William Cardinal O'Connell.

crony John F. Fitzgerald, then mayor of Boston, had presented his daughter Rose to society. Joe Kennedy had known Rose since early childhood and had hopes of marrying her, but the man he hoped would be his father-in-law, "Honey Fitz," took a dim view of such an eventuality. For one thing, the Fitzgeralds were rising socially and had every intention of rising even higher. For another, P. J. Kennedy, despite origins that were no more impressive than Honey Fitz's, had taken few pains over the years to hide his contempt for the other man's raffish manner and egocentric behavior. Joe Kennedy's sudden rise to a bank presidency put a different coloration on matters, though; Rose Fitzgerald and Joseph P. Kennedy were married in October, 1914.

Like Joe Kennedy's grandfather Patrick, Rose's grandfather Thomas had emigrated from County Wexford to Boston, where he found work as a common laborer. Unlike Patrick Kennedy, though, Thomas Fitzgerald prospered—at least by the standards of the Irish North End—and by the time John Francis, the third of his seven sons, was born, he owned his own grocery and liquor store. Surprisingly—almost astonishingly for a first-generation Irish boy—John Francis, like Joe Kennedy a generation later, attended Boston Latin, where the likes of George Santayana and Bernard Berenson were preparing themselves for the life of the mind. Surprisingly, too, he entered Harvard Medical School on graduating from Boston Latin, but dropped out after a year, when his father died. During the next few years, John Francis worked as a clerk in the Boston Custom House, familiarized himself with the mechanics of the civil service, and then resigned to go into the insurance business in his native North End. Glib-tongued and boosterish, he joined every joinable Catholic organization and whatever non-denominational fraternities would have him, earned himself the sobriquet "Fitzblarney," and, at twenty-six, married one of Boston's prettier colleens, Josephine Mary Hannon.

Like P. J. Kennedy, Johnny Fitz (as he was also known) soon went into politics and in short order was so indisputably the boss of Ward Six that he had earned himself still another nickname, The North End Napoleon. With the backing of the most powerful boss of them all, Martin Lomasney, Johnny Fitz's career advanced apace. But when a triumvirate of Irish bosses (of whom P. J. Kennedy was one) offered to admit Johnny to their circle with the proviso that he dissociate himself from Lomasney, he spurned his old protector. Ten years later, modestly having dubbed himself *Shawn A. Boo,* or "John the Bold," Fitzgerald was elected mayor of Boston after staging the most spectacular campaign in the city's history. John the Bold (who was finally to be remembered as Honey Fitz) then attempted to turn staid old Boston into a sort of Fun City—it was estimated that during his first term in office he danced with no fewer than five thousand girls—to the detriment of Rose's social ambitions.

Joe Kennedy continued to make money, proceeded to father a family of nine children, and made something of a name for himself as a local institution. He was covered by the newspapers, according to an editor of the Boston *Post,* "almost the way we covered City Hospital and the courts." With the entry of the United States into the first World War, Joe, who had taken over as assistant manager of the Fore River shipyard, a subsidiary of Bethlehem Steel, set all sorts of production records and in no way diminished his personal fortune in the process.

As the Kennedy family proliferated (a son, Joe Junior, was born in July of 1915; John Fitzgerald, in May, 1917; Rosemary, in 1919; Kathleen, in 1920), Joe and Rose Kennedy moved from their frame house in Brookline to a twelve-room establishment on Naples Road. Another daughter, Eunice, was born in 1921, and still another, Patricia, in 1924.

In 1922, Joe's father-in-law, Honey Fitz (who in the meantime had been unseated from a fraudulently obtained seat in the United States Congress), made a final try for higher elective office and was swamped by a gubernatorial candidate whom he had outrageously slandered in the campaign's closing days. The first-generation Fitzgeralds and Kennedys had gone as far, politically, as they could go, and it remained for Joe Kennedy and his heirs to build a superstructure on the dynastic foundations that P. J. and Honey Fitz had laid. Such a dynasty would depend for its viability on the males fathered by Joe Kennedy.

A third son, Robert Francis, was born to Joe and Rose Kennedy on November 20, 1925.

A few years before Robert's birth, Rose Kennedy posed with Eunice, Kathleen, Rosemary, Jack, and Joe.

Chapter 2

FAMILY SOLIDARITY

Tell me, when are the nice people of Boston going to accept us?
— ROSE KENNEDY

Well, Rose, this is a helluva long way from East Boston, isn't it?
—JOSEPH P. KENNEDY, SR.
(while dressing for dinner at Windsor Castle)

In the spring of 1926, when Robert Kennedy was six months old, Joe moved his family to Riverdale, a quiet upper-middle-class residential area overlooking the Hudson River in the Bronx. The reasons for the move were mixed, but it was made primarily because Joe Kennedy had at long last reconciled himself to the bitter truth that an Irish Catholic family would never be altogether acceptable in the higher social circles of Yankee Boston. He had gone to the right schools, true, and had been more than merely tolerated at them—but less than fully accepted; he had never, for example, been admitted to the "best" undergraduate clubs. Both his father and Rose's might wield considerable power in the city, but as far as Boston's Brahmins were concerned, it was not who *you* were that counted but who your forebears were. As Ralph Lowell, a Harvard contemporary of impeccable origins, put it years later, "It was petty and cruel. The women in Cohasset [a summer colony popular with proper Bostonians] looked down on the daughter of 'Honey Fitz'; and who was Joe Kennedy but the son of Pat, the barkeeper?"

Joe once remarked that "Boston is a good city to come from, not a good city to go to. If you want to make money, go where the money is." But while his departure from the Hub was motivated in part by his search for larger financial worlds to conquer, the main reason for the move was simply that life for an Irish Catholic in well-to-do Brookline was in its own way as intolerable as was the life of an Irishman in the festering slums of East Boston. "I felt Catholic Boston was no place to bring up Catholic children," Joe explained years later. He might have added that except for a measure of physical comfort, Protestant Boston was worse. "They wouldn't have asked my daughters to join their debutante clubs," he remarked testily, and added (with a touch of sour grapes): "Not that our girls would have joined anyway. . . ." Many years later, Robert Kennedy was to tell a South African audience about a system of apartheid not much less onerous than South Africa's own. "My father left Boston, Massachusetts," he said, "because of the signs on the wall that said, 'No Irish Need Apply.' "

As it turned out, Riverdale was not a vast improvement on Brookline, and neither was the nearby Westchester community of Bronxville, to which

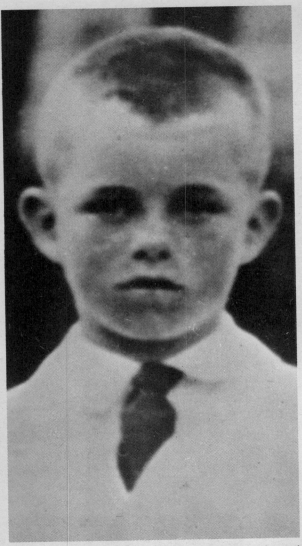

Bobby Kennedy was nine years old and a resident of Bronxville, New York, when this photograph was taken.

Joseph P. Kennedy, Sr. moved his family in 1929.

The money rolled in, but the neighbors remained aloof; not for the usual reasons, but simply because the Kennedys were strangers—and who wouldn't be diffident about forcing his company on an obviously well-heeled stranger? The Kennedys turned increasingly inward. Family solidarity became the substitute for a social life. "Years ago," Rose Kennedy was to recall long afterward, "we decided that our children were going to be our best friends and that we could never see too much of them. Since we couldn't do both, it was better to bring up our family than go out to dinners." Just how many dinner invitations the elder Kennedys received is not a matter of record. As Margaret Laing, a biographer of Robert Kennedy, remarked, however, "Luckily there were enough of them for their isolation to be disguised, and in some ways turned to their own advantage."

Joseph P. Kennedy doted on all his children, but particularly on his eldest son, Joe. Bobby, ten years younger than Joe, and Jack's junior by eight years, profited less from his brothers' company than from the example they—and especially Joe—set. (The fourth Kennedy son, Edward, was born in 1932.) As John F. Kennedy later wrote: "If the Kennedy children amount to anything . . . it will be due more to Joe's behavior and his constant example than to any other factor. He made the task of bringing up a large family immeasurably easier for my father and mother, for what they taught him he passed on to us and their teachings were not diluted through him but rather strengthened." Joe Junior's role as a conductor of parental precepts was of particular importance during Bobby's early years because his father, then very much involved with the movie industry, spent a good deal of his time on the West Coast.

Young Bobby was the runt of the Kennedy litter. "He was the smallest and thinnest," according to his mother, "and we feared he might grow up puny and girlish." That Bobby himself might have entertained similar fears is indicated by John Kennedy's earliest memory of his sibling—a memory of a freckled four-year-old trying to emulate his brother Joe by flinging himself into deep water off Hyannis Port when he could barely swim. Whether the performance showed "a lot of guts or no sense at all," remarked the late President, depended "on how you looked at it."

Business permitting, Joe Kennedy, Sr. delegated little authority where the education of his children was concerned. As Margaret Laing notes, "On the occasions when Joseph Kennedy was at home from Palm Beach or California or wherever else his various interests were currently taking him, mealtimes were study sessions. It was an ideal opportunity: all the children were gathered together for once, and the dining room became a lecture hall."

The burden of Joseph P. Kennedy's lectures to his progeny can be summed up in one word: "Win." Whatever the game might be, winning was its name. "I don't think much of people who have it in them to be first, but who finish second," was the way he put it. "If you've got a second choice, then you haven't got a first choice." Although football was a major Kennedy interest, it is improbable that Grantland Rice's poem "Alumnus Football"—with its reference to the "One Great Scorer" who "marks—not that you won or lost—but how you played the game"—seemed any more manly or instructive to Old Joe than did the "Ode to a Nightingale."

The Kennedys were a crowd in themselves, but it is quite possible to be lonely in a crowd, and young Bobby, isolated chronologically from his three brothers by a gaggle of sisters, became increasingly moody and withdrawn. Moreover, the friendships he might normally have made during a healthy, active childhood failed to materialize because he often changed schools. As a nine-year-old, he was described by a friend of Jack's as "a hell of a nice little boy, one of the nicest I ever met. He was always responsible, friendly, and thoughtful." As the years went by, however, the friendliness became less apparent and the niceness (at least according to his more vehement detractors), all but invisible. Those who knew him best, though, were inclined to see in him not hostility but shyness.

Of the Kennedy boys, young Bobby most resembled his father. ("He's a great kid," Old Joe blurted out on one occasion. "He hates the same way I do"—a remark that was to haunt the Kennedys, *pere et fils,* for years to come.) Like his father before him, a young Bobby beaten on the playing field was always good for an awesome dis-

In 1939, when Joe Kennedy was Ambassador to the
Court of St. James's, he took his family to Rome for

a special audience with the Pope. Bobby stands fourth from the left in this photograph taken at Vatican City.

play of pyrotechnics. "I remember watching Bobby playing tennis with my children at Palm Beach," an old family acquaintance recalls. "He lost, and threw the racket down in a rage." And like his father, he showed little aptitude for academic pursuits. Unlike Joe Senior, however, he made up in sheer doggedness for what he lacked in natural ability during his school years. "He didn't attend school," a classmate of his prep school years recalled, "he attacked it"; and the dean of Milton Academy characterized him as "not a naturally brilliant student, who just flicked off the grades. He had to work. . . ."

As it did to his father, religion meant a great deal to him—more perhaps than to his brothers—and after entertaining such predictable ambitions as the life of a fire chief or a streetcar conductor, he thought (quite seriously while in his teens) of becoming a priest. And like his father, he had something of an entrepreneurial streak: at one point he tried breeding rabbits commercially, and then had a brief fling at magazine distribution. (In contrast to Joe Senior, who had made his youthful business rounds as a nonpaying trolley passenger, young Robert, with more style than acumen, delivered his goods in the family Rolls-Royce.)

Meanwhile, Joe Kennedy, Sr. was wheeling and dealing on a grander scale than ever before. He made millions in a variety of enterprises, sometimes "in a very roundabout way," came through the crash of 1929 in fine financial fettle, backed Franklin Delano Roosevelt with a great deal of ardency, won himself a couple of New Deal posts, and—to the openmouthed dismay of the Secretary of State, Cordell Hull, was appointed Ambassador to the Court of St. James's in 1938. At this point he began entertaining visions of himself as the first Roman Catholic President of the United States. As ambassador, however, he advocated policies with which Roosevelt and most Americans did not agree, made a number of ill-advised statements, and finally resigned in disfavor in December, 1940.

The second generation, however, had gone far indeed. It now remained for the third to go all the way, and to that end Joseph P. Kennedy, Jr. was already being groomed. As the eldest son he *must* one day fulfill his father's dream of a Catholic President. And should anything go awry, John, as second eldest, was next in line of succession. "The eldest, Joe Junior," decreed Old Joe, "will study at the Harvard Law School; Jack will work at the Harvard Business School. It does not necessarily mean," he added slyly, "that they will become a lawyer and businessman, respectively." Whatever his plans may have been for Bobby, he didn't bother to enunciate them at the time.

By the time Bobby was fourteen, the first Kennedy of his generation, big brother Joe, had made his entry into politics as a delegate to the Democratic National Convention of 1940, where he adamantly backed James A. Farley although the delegation's chairman switched *his* support from Farley to a third term for Franklin D. Roosevelt. The first deliberate step in Old Joe's Grand Design to put a Catholic (and more specifically, a Kennedy) into the White House was thus taken. Politics dominated the thoughts of the Kennedy boys that campaign summer of 1940 more than ever before. Even young Bobby, whose particular attachment to his brother Jack had become more marked as he moved into his teens, was beginning to take a lively interest in the affairs of the world—an interest somewhat more genuine than that stimulated by his father's compulsory dinner-table lectures.

After briefly attending a Catholic school in Rhode Island, Bobby was enrolled in a posh prep school, Milton Academy, outside Boston. The experience, like most of his school experiences, was not particularly happy. Intensely introverted in his late teens, he was, according to a classmate, "no good at small talk . . . no good at social amenities, [and] no great lover."

With the United States at war, Joe Kennedy, Jr. and his brother Jack were both in the Navy, and Bobby, who had entered college, was enrolled in a Navy V-12 Training Unit at Harvard. "I have four boys," Joe Kennedy had remarked in 1936, "and I don't want them to be killed in a foreign war." One of those boys, Jack, narrowly missed suffering such a fate when his PT boat was sunk in the Pacific in August of 1943. Then, a year later, the thing Joe Kennedy most dreaded happened: Joe Junior, the scion of the rising dynasty, was blown to bits while flying a load of explosives over the English Channel. Old Joe's grief was unassuageable. For a father who was to have tragedy visited upon him with appalling regularity, this first was to remain the

Bobby was smaller and slower than most of the boys on Harvard's football team, but he was determined to make the varsity, and he did. At left, he receives a pass. Below, he and teammates relax.

most terrible of fate's blows. For Robert Kennedy, it was an unwelcome move upward in the line of succession.

Determined to become the family's third war hero, Bobby used some parental influence to obtain his release from Harvard's officers' training program and assignment to active duty as a seaman second class aboard the newly commissioned destroyer, the *Joseph P. Kennedy, Jr.* To his intense chagrin, the war ended before he could see action. Bobby (who years later was to maintain that except for war, football was life's best school) returned to college, where most of his energies seem to have been expended on the football field.

An occasional slightly built quarterback notwithstanding, football is a big man's game. At about five feet ten and one hundred and fifty pounds, Bobby lacked the basic physical equipment for the game. Moreover, he was slow afoot. Kenny O'Donnell, who captained the Harvard varsity squad (and who was to remain a lifelong friend of Bobby's), later recalled that although he at first had absolutely no right to make the team, Kennedy "just *made* himself better." On November 22, 1947, Bob Kennedy sat on the Harvard bench nursing a heavily bandaged leg. Yale had a commanding lead and the clock had almost run out. Perhaps remembering the apoplectic rage Old Man Kennedy had flown into when his son Joe Junior wasn't allowed into the Yale game in *his* senior year, coach Dick Harlow waved the Kennedy kid onto the field for the last few plays. Characteristically, the runt of the Ken-

During World War II, Joe Kennedy, Jr. (above right) was killed in action in Europe, and Jack became a hero in the Pacific Theater. Bobby enlisted in the Navy. Below, Joe Senior watches proudly as his son is sworn in.

nedy family was the only one of Old Joe's first three sons to win his letter.

As aggressive as he may have been on the field, Bobby was inordinately shy once he had doffed his shoulder pads. "He was very quiet," one of his contemporaries later remembered. "He didn't drink; he didn't smoke; he didn't date many girls—very, very few." Not smoking or drinking paid off handsomely. On his twenty-first birthday Bobby received a thousand-dollar check from his father for his abstemiousness.

Immediately after his graduation, Bobby Kennedy left for Palestine, where he spent the summer of 1948 covering the Arab-Jewish hostilities as a correspondent for the Boston *Post*. The Israelis, he cabled his paper, "are a young, tough, determined nation." "They fight," he added, "with unparalleled courage. This is their greatest and last chance; there will be no turning back." At one point during his stint as a war reporter, an Israeli convoy in which he planned to travel to Jerusalem was wiped out by a very tough, determined body of Arabs. Kennedy finally reached Jerusalem with the aid of an Israeli captain.

Conditions in Jerusalem at the time were chaotic. Arabs were fleeing their own quarter and settling, destitute of their possessions, in the Old City, there to brood on the fortunes of war. One such Arab was Bishara Sirhan, a relatively well-off civil service official who abruptly found himself unemployed and with several mouths to feed. His young son Sirhan was four years old.

Chapter 3

A BUSINESS FULL OF KNIVES

And how could I get up there and denounce Joe McCarthy when my own brother was working for him?
— JOHN F. KENNEDY

On applying for admission to the University of Virginia Law School in 1948, Robert F. Kennedy laconically gave his reason for not re-entering Harvard as "graduation"; to which an interested observer later retorted, "He'd never have turned it [Harvard Law School] down if he could have gone there."

At Virginia, he plodded away at his studies in lackluster fashion. He had "lots on the ball," according to his professor of labor law, "but he would never set the Thames on fire scholastically. . . . He had an understanding of labor relations all right. How much he understands of the finer points of law is debatable. . . ."

Kennedy may not have acquired an intimate knowledge of law while at Virginia, but he did acquire a reputation as an analyst of world affairs, thanks to an uncommonly good paper on the Yalta settlement, and a reputation as a fighter for his principles. He also acquired a wife.

Ethel Skakel, who had been a roommate of Jean Kennedy's at Manhattanville College of the Sacred Heart in New York's Westchester County, first met Bobby during a ski vacation at Mont Tremblant in 1944, and immediately set her cap for him ("I thought he was divine," she averred later). In June, 1950, they were married in St. Mary's Church in Greenwich, Connecticut.

Back in Charlottesville after honeymooning in Hawaii, the newlyweds rented an off-campus house, and according to an acquaintance, "entertained a good deal." Of Bobby, the same observer noted with some significance that "he had few friends." He did have a number of admirers, though, chiefly because of his activities as president of the Student Legal Forum. In this role, Bobby made good use of his father's connections. A stream of dignitaries appeared as guest speakers at Bobby's behest, although at least one of them had trouble maintaining his dignity: "Get that dog out of here!" bellowed Senator Joseph McCarthy when a mongrel, for reasons best known to itself, made its way purposefully toward the podium.

The most revealing—and by far the most praiseworthy—of Bob Kennedy's accomplishments during his tenure as president of the Forum involved a bitter fight over a scheduled appearance by Dr. Ralph Bunche, who had accepted an invitation to speak to the students with the proviso that the Virginia audience be integrated. Bobby, according to a Forum committee member, "blew his stack" at the Southern students who rebelled against signing a resolution favoring the integration they approved of in principle. "He was so mad he could hardly talk. He had a lack of understanding of the problems these people faced; to him it seemed illogical to support something but be unwilling to sign for it." Bobby carried his fight to the president of the university after rejecting a compromise solution, and Bunche spoke to an integrated audience. It had been Bobby's first big fight on a matter of principle and he had won.

In entering law school, Bobby Kennedy had followed the course of least resistance: "I wanted to do graduate work, but I didn't know whether to go to law school or business school. I had no attraction to business, so I entered law school." Once out of law school, however, he had a better idea of what he was about and applied for an appointment to the Justice Department "because I wanted to go into the government." His government service began in 1951 with a $4,200-a-year post in the department's Internal Security Division. (It might be noted at this juncture that Joe Kennedy, Sr. had been at pains to ensure his children's freedom from any financial concern whatever, and that the question of remuneration in no case had any bearing on the choice of a career.)

One concern of the Internal Security Division at that time was an admission by John Peurifoy, an

Bobby and Ethel leave St. Mary's Church in Greenwich, Connecticut, after their wedding on June 17, 1950.

assistant secretary of state, that ninety-one homosexuals had been fired from his department as security risks. This naturally led to some conjecture about how many more similarly oriented types might still be on the State Department's payroll, and Kennedy was given the job of sifting through the Justice Department's voluminous files on suspected risks. Before long, however, he was transferred to the department's Criminal Division and was assigned to the United States Attorney's office in New York, which was then in the process of gathering evidence of corruption in the Truman administration. Whatever tales Joe Kennedy, Sr. may have told his son about ward politics in Boston apparently had been expurgated to the point where they sounded like a high-school civics course. At any rate, the somewhat ingenuous Bobby's first glimpses of political corruption seem to have come as something of an eye-opener to him, and in the words of a biographer, Charles Guggenheim, "set the course of his life for the next ten years."

Bobby was momentarily deflected from that course almost before he had embarked on it. In 1952, he left the Justice Department with some reluctance to run his brother Jack's campaign for a seat in the United States Senate. "He didn't want to work in the '52 campaign," according to a friend. "He had become excited by cases he was involved in. It was totally against his will to come and work in the campaign. But nobody else could have done it but a member of the family." (Stated that simply, the assertion may be misleading. Others *could* possibly have done it. The question was whether Jack Kennedy, with his paternally inspired don't-trust-anyone-but-family outlook, would have *wanted* others doing it.)

Despite the closeness of the Kennedy family, Bobby and Jack had hardly known each other as young children. There had been, in their own miniaturized scheme of things, what amounted to a generation gap between them. Now, as adults with a common purpose, an eight-year age difference no longer mattered. More than just a political campaign was forged in that summer and fall of 1952; a bond was established that was inexorably to change not only the course of Robert Kennedy's life, but the man himself. But nobody—and least of all Bobby—could know it at the time. He endeared himself to no one that fall. "I'm not running a popularity contest," he snarled. "It doesn't matter whether they like me or not. Jack can be nice to them." "Them" referred to his own staff members in this case, but might accurately have applied to anyone in the state. At one point during the campaign, Old Joe Kennedy was told by Massachusetts Governor Paul Dever: "I know you're an important man around here and all that, but I'm telling you this and I mean it. Keep that fresh kid of yours out of my sight from here on in."

Not just one, but three Kennedys beat Henry Cabot Lodge in an election year in which Dwight Eisenhower carried many a Republican to victory on his coattails. Officially, Jack was Lodge's Democratic opponent, but Old Joe, who had all but forced

In 1953, R.F.K. became an assistant counsel for Joseph McCarthy's Permanent Investigations Subcommittee. (Above, he confers with McCarthy, center, and Senator Stuart Symington.) "No real spadework that might have destroyed some of their pet theories was ever undertaken," Bobby wrote later about McCarthy and his staff.

his son into the race ("When you've beaten him you've beaten the best"), and brash young Bobby seemed to be everywhere, and to be doing everything, at once. "It was," wrote the political analysts Ralph G. Martin and Ed Plaut, "the most methodical . . . the most intricate, the most disciplined and smoothly working statewide campaign in Massachusetts history—and possibly anywhere else." And another observer, a Republican, blamed his candidate's downfall not on Jack, but on "that family of his . . . they're all over the state."

With his victory over Lodge, John F. Kennedy had taken a giant step toward the realization of Old Joe's plans. And Bobby had taken a giant step of his own. For the next eleven years, the two brothers would be marching almost as one. "They didn't become really close until 1952," observed their sister Eunice Shriver, " and it was politics that brought them together. That's a business full of knives. Jack needed someone he could trust, someone who had loyalty to him. Jack knew he had a person like that with Bobby around."

His brother was safely installed in the Senate, but his victory, as Old Joe put it, left Bobby "unemployed." Then, with a variety of possibilities open to him, he opted for a post on the staff of Senator Joseph McCarthy's Permanent Investigations Subcommittee. It was not the most prudent choice he could have made.

Joe McCarthy was an old family friend of the Kennedys', and one who had already caused them (not to mention the country at large) no little embarrassment (it was rumored that Joe Kennedy, Sr. had bribed the Wisconsin Republican to stay out of Massachusetts during Jack's senatorial campaign; Old Joe admitted that three thousand dollars had changed hands at a critical moment, but denied that it was a bribe). A bully and a demagogue—and quite a charmer withal—McCarthy was already in bad odor in both the Senate and liberal circles in and out of government when Kennedy went to work for him.

Kennedy remained on McCarthy's staff for only six months; by then, the senator's henchman-in-chief, Roy Cohn, was more than he could take. Although they were exactly equal in terms of seniority, Cohn was chief counsel, Kennedy, only assistant counsel. Whether it was having to play second fiddle that really bothered Kennedy most is a debatable point. On his own say-so, Bobby was dissatisfied with the state of affairs because "most of the investigations [by Cohn and his side-kick G. David Schine] were instituted on the basis of some preconceived notion by the chief counsel or his staff members and not on the basis of any information that had been developed. . . . I thought Senator McCarthy made a mistake in allowing the Committee to operate in such a fashion." In any case he tendered his resignation to the senator—who also happened to be the godfather of his and Ethel's first child, Kathleen, born in 1951. McCarthy praised his departing employee as "a great credit to the committee" during his six months' stay.

Although Bobby had left the subcommittee's

By 1957, Ethel and Bobby were the parents of five children. Joseph is feeding the pony in this picture, while

Ethel holds six-month-old Mary Courtney. In the cart (left to right) are Kathleen, Robert Jr., and David.

legal staff ostensibly to enter private practice, he soon turned up on the Hoover Commission, of which Joe Kennedy, Sr. was a member. Six months later he had resigned once more and had taken a post with Senator John McClellan of Arkansas, also a friend of his father's and a minority member of McCarthy's subcommittee. He had joined McClellan's staff as an "adviser" just in time to participate in one of the most bizarre episodes in the long, bizarre history of American politics: the Army-McCarthy hearings. And who should turn out to be the villain of the piece—aside of course from McCarthy himself—but Kennedy's old adversary Roy Cohn! While the television cameras explored the Wisconsin senator's thinly thatched pate, and the microphones relayed his endlessly iterated foghorn call of "Point of order, Mr. Chairman" to a mesmerized nationwide audience; while a Yankee lawyer named Joseph Welch wept as gleefully as an oyster-eating Carpenter, and the Secretary of the Army put on a masterful impersonation of a ribbon clerk who had somehow got himself entangled with a Rocky Marciano, Robert Kennedy and Roy Cohn slugged it out in the wings (almost literally on one occasion). It was a fairly even match. They were both young, both brash, both tough. In the end, the consensus was that Bobby had won a split decision.

The main-eventer, McCarthy, though, had been soundly beaten, and the dossier on Cohn compiled by Bobby helped beat him. (Still, when the broken, alcoholic McCarthy died in 1957, Bobby journeyed to Wisconsin to mourn him.)

At the 1956 Democratic convention, Jack Kennedy lost the vice-presidential nomination on the third ballot.

McCarthy was censured by his Senate colleagues in December, 1954. The following month, with a Democratic majority back in the Senate, John McClellan became chairman of the subcommittee and appointed Bobby its chief counsel. Bobby, who had objected more to McCarthy's and Cohn's methods than to what many considered their madness, continued to investigate alleged irregularities in the military.

The liberalization of Robert Kennedy began during a trip to the Soviet Union in the company of Justice William O. Douglas, in 1955. While traveling through Siberia, Bobby suddenly became very ill (Douglas' layman's diagnosis was "probably pneumonia"), lapsed into unconsciousness for a while, and lost considerable weight. By the time the trip was finished, he had also lost a few black-and-white notions regarding the inhabitants of the Communist world. "The trip," Justice Douglas later recalled, ". . . shook him up." The gist of Douglas' further remarks was that if a Russian lady doctor could save an American's life, Communism couldn't be all that evil.

The following year Bobby tried—against his better judgment—to steer Jack into the vice-presidential nomination that Estes Kefauver finally won ("I told [Jack that losing] was the luckiest thing that ever happened to him"). Then, in 1957, he embarked on an almost monomaniacal big game hunt that was not to end until a decade later, and was to earn him a reputation for ruthlessness that he was never quite able to live down.

Chapter 4

GOING FOR THE JUGULAR

He's a young, dim-witted, curly-headed smart aleck.
—JAMES RIDDLE HOFFA

Clear it with Bobby.
—JOHN F. KENNEDY

At the age of thirty-one, Robert F. Kennedy was the father of five children and a veteran of a couple of political wars; he had held a variety of jobs in government—and he was still relatively little known to the nation at large. To most Americans, mention of the name "Kennedy" might call to mind the junior senator from Massachusetts, the former ambassador, or the movie comedian (Edgar Kennedy) who specialized in the slow burn. In the next few years, however, Robert Kennedy was to establish a reputation in his own right, and then, as his brother's alter ego, was to be generally recognized as the second most powerful figure in the nation.

The Senate's Select Committee on Improper Activities in the Labor and Management Field (commonly and less euphemistically called the Rackets

Above, at a meeting of the Senate Labor Rackets Committee are Senators Pat McNamara, Barry Goldwater, and John McClellan with R.F.K. Below, Bobby uses a chart to explain the financial deals of Teamsters Union President Dave Beck. His efforts to jail Beck's successor, James Hoffa (right), did not succeed until 1967.

Committee) was formed in 1957, largely on the basis of evidence supplied by Robert Kennedy. The year before, it had been suggested to Kennedy by the newsman Clark Mollenhoff, a reporter for the Cowles newspapers, that an investigation of the International Brotherhood of Teamsters, Chauffeurs, Warehousemen, and Helpers of America might turn up some interesting information. After hesitating momentarily, Kennedy undertook some preliminary spadework and discovered that the activities of the Teamsters Union exuded the aroma of an overdue mackerel trawler. Kennedy presented his findings to Senator McClellan, and the Rackets Committee was formed, with Bobby as chief counsel.

The first target was Teamsters President Dave Beck, who proved to be an easy mark. Beck, it seems, had some unusually refined proclivities for a man who headed an organization largely composed of truck drivers. He was, among other things, a lover of flowers. Or so it was alleged: $320,000 in union funds—if the committee's suspicions were not unfounded—had been used to defray the costs of some gardening Beck had had done around his home. During the hearings that followed, a strangely gentle accord obtained between the horticulturist and his inquisitor:

KENNEDY: Do you feel that if you gave a truthful answer to this Committee on your taking of $320,000 of Union funds that that might tend to incriminate you?

BECK: It might.

KENNEDY: Is that right?

BECK: It might.

KENNEDY: I feel the same way.

Kennedy's tone grew somewhat sharper as the hearings went on. Frustrated again and again by witnesses seeking refuge behind the Fifth Amendment, his questioning took on a savage, hectoring quality that in no way enhanced the decorum of the committee hearings, and that contributed in no small part to Bobby's growing reputation for ruthlessness. To a Chicagoan who preferred silence to possible incrimination, he snarled, "You haven't got the guts . . . have you Mr. Glimco?" Mr. Glimco was then informed that he was morally "kind of yellow inside." Occasionally, there were moments of high comedy, although Bobby was by this time so steamed up that he may not have appreciated them:

KENNEDY: Did you know Cockeye Dunne?

BARNEY BAKER (a Teamsters organizer): I didn't know him as Cockeye Dunne; I knew him as John Dunne.

KENNEDY: Where is he now?

BAKER: He has met his maker.

KENNEDY: How did he do that?

BAKER: I believe through electrocution in the city of New York of the state of New York.

Dave Beck was convicted of grand larceny and income tax evasion by the end of the year, and resigned as president of the union. He was replaced by James Riddle Hoffa, who proved to be a much tougher opponent. By this time, however, Robert Kennedy had become a very tough fellow himself; so tough that an impressed Teamsters member re-

Above, Bobby, Teddy, and Jack confer in California during the 1960 presidential campaign, in which Kennedy solidarity (and money) proved to be an invaluable asset. While he was serving in the Senate, J.F.K. had once remarked, "Just as I went into politics because Joe died, if anything happened to me tomorrow my brother Bobby would run for my seat in the Senate. And if Bobby died, Teddy would take over for him."

marked that if he could find nothing else to say of Bobby, he had to admit that he and Hoffa deserved each other. Whether it was his principles or simply his desire to win that most motivated Bobby in his pursuit of Hoffa is still being debated. Recognizing a worthy opponent, the toughest he had ever had, the slim, boyish chief counsel went after the squat, hard-nosed labor leader as though his very life depended on the outcome. On the surface, Hoffa appeared much more relaxed than Kennedy, and even joshed his antagonist for "dirtying government property" when at one point Kennedy put his feet on a chair. Beneath the superficial jocularity, though, another Jimmy Hoffa knew that he *was* fighting for his life—at least, a life on the sweeter side of penitentiary walls—and *that* Jimmy Hoffa was not about to be beaten by a brat millionaire's son who had gotten his job ("This is a lawyer?") through "nepotism."

Kennedy was merciless in his baiting of Hoffa and his forgetful colleagues, and was so convinced of eventual victory that he offered to jump off the Capitol dome if he lost. His methods were questionable enough to evoke the concern of civil libertarians, one of whom, a Yale law professor, was to accuse him of conducting "purely punitive expeditions," of "relentless vindictive battering" of the witnesses, and of unethical inferences of guilt. In the end, Hoffa was acquitted. His lawyer offered Bobby the use of a parachute.

In 1959, just after the birth of his seventh child, Kennedy resigned from the Rackets Committee to write *The Enemy Within,* a book in which he continued to shadowbox with Hoffa.

Bobby Kennedy had little time in which to brood over his defeat. A far bigger fight was now shaping up, one in which defeat was unthinkable. John F. Kennedy—a century after his great-grandfather Patrick had died obscurely in a noisome East Boston slum—had decided to run for the most powerful elective office on earth.

If Jack Kennedy's misconceived attempt at the 1956 vice-presidential nomination (an attempt to which Old Joe had been unalterably opposed) had achieved nothing else, it had taught him—and Bobby—some valuable political lessons. They had learned, for one thing, that politics is largely a game of intangibles, of timing, of enthusiasm, and not simply cold tactics. Adlai Stevenson's losing campaign of that year had taught them further lessons. As a mere assistant and liaison man in that ultimately swamped venture, Bobby had had little to do but acquaint himself with the intricacies of inefficiency. "I had time to watch everything," he later remarked. "I was learning what not to do." The brothers had also learned that—as their father had been telling them all their lives—there was no point in settling for a second choice: even had Jack won the vice-presidential nomination, the Eisenhower landslide would probably have smashed his political future along with Adlai Stevenson's. Even before Stevenson's debacle, John Kennedy had stated: "I'm not running for Vice-President anymore. I'm now running for President."

As the Kennedy effort shaped up, it became clear that the candidate would, insofar as it was possible, maintain the fiction that he was above participation in "a business full of knives." The dirtier aspects of Jack's presidential campaign would be left to his brother Bobby. "Bobby Kennedy," wrote columnist Murray Kempton, "goes around saying that Jimmy Hoffa will spend anything to beat Jack. This statement does not say outright that Hoffa is contributing money to poor Humphrey, but what other inference is possible?" Kempton went on to describe Bobby as "sharp, tough and clever." Hubert Humphrey himself, who was engaged in a series of presidential primary battles with Jack, alluded to Bobby's growing reputation as a sore loser when he said: "Politics is a serious business, not a boy's game where you can pick up your ball and run home if things don't go according to your idea of who should win." Bobby, however, was well aware of the seriousness of the business at hand. It was just that he had no intention of having things not go according to his idea of who should win—and he certainly had no intention of picking up his ball and running home like a boy.

The West Virginia primary was crucial to John F. Kennedy's campaign for the Presidency, and Bobby Kennedy fought it savagely, constantly falling back on his *idée fixe,* the perfidious James Riddle Hoffa. Hoffa, he intimated, had ordered the West Virginia Teamsters to support Humphrey because of his personal vendetta with the Kennedys. "This is just cheap, lowdown gutter politics,"

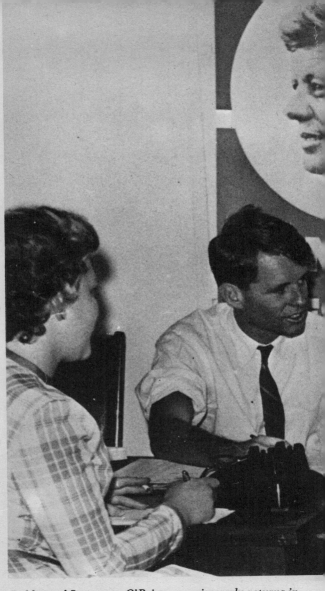

Bobby and Lawrence O'Brien appraise early returns in the West Virginia primary of May, 1960. Jack Ken-

nedy's victory over Senator Hubert Humphrey proved that he could win the votes of nonaffluent Protestants.

snapped Humphrey, who then went on to accuse Bobby of McCarthyist tactics and election buying. To the latter charge, Jack Kennedy quipped: "I got a wire from my father that said, 'Dear Jack. Don't buy one more vote than necessary. I'll be damned if I'll pay for a landslide.' " The wisecrack drew a laugh from his audience—which happened to be in New York—but in West Virginia and elsewhere the charge was no laughing matter. One West Virginia newspaper editor called the election "one of the most corrupt" in his county's history. The West Virginia campaign was Bobby's campaign, and nobody knew it better than Robert Francis Kennedy. When it was over, and Hubert Humphrey had been knocked out of contention, a jubilant Bobby cracked: "I couldn't have done it without my brother."

If Bobby was rough on the opposition, he treated his brother's supporters no more gently. "Win, win, win" had been his father's only precept, and it had included no qualifying adjectives like "gracefully." "Gentlemen," John Kennedy's campaign manager bluntly told a group of Democrats, "I don't give a damn if the state and county organizations survive after November, and I don't give a damn if *you* survive. I want to elect John F. Kennedy." It all fitted in perfectly with one of Old Joe Kennedy's favorite mottoes: "When the going gets tough, the tough get going."

It would be a mistake to imagine that John Kennedy's 1960 campaign depended for its force solely on Robert Kennedy's roughness. Bobby's quip

Bobby's intervention on behalf of Martin Luther King, jailed in Georgia, won Negro votes for J.F.K. in 1960.

about his brother's minor role in his own candidacy notwithstanding, Jack Kennedy was very much his own man. Politics *is* a business full of knives, though, and Jack was astute enough to know that his image would not be much enhanced if he did the cutting-up himself. And Bobby was the only man he trusted to do it for him. Nor was Bobby's role in the campaign confined solely to doing Jack's dirty work. The Kennedy campaign was a masterful exercise in organization and attention to detail. ("It's the best organization job I've ever seen in politics," crowed Joe Kennedy, Sr. when it was all over.) Much of the credit for that job was Robert Kennedy's. "Jack works as hard as any mortal man can," Old Joe remarked on another occasion. "Bobby goes a little farther."

Jack Kennedy had been nominated on the first ballot at the Democratic National Convention in Los Angeles. He was just one step away from the fulfillment of his father's lifelong dream. It was, however, an enormous step, and the ground was slippery. The choice of a vice-presidential nominee was of crucial importance: it would have to be a man who could offset the unpopularity of a Catholic candidate in the South. Ultimately, Jack Kennedy's choice of Lyndon B. Johnson was proved sound. The choice could have been made more gracefully, though, and the clumsiness with which Johnson was offered the second spot on the ticket was partly due to Bobby Kennedy's immaturity.

Lyndon Johnson had once slightingly and with some accuracy referred to Joe Kennedy, Sr. as a

"Chamberlain umbrella man," and Bobby had never forgiven him for it. Now Bobby was in Johnson's hotel suite, supposedly to find out whether the Texan had decided to accept Jack's offer of second spot on the ticket. Accounts conflict on what happened next, but at one point the late Phil Graham, publisher of the Washington *Post* and of *Newsweek,* found himself on the telephone to the presidential candidate, informing him that Bobby was telling ". . . Lyndon that there is opposition and that Lyndon should withdraw." Somehow the confusion was smoothed over, and Johnson's acceptance was obtained despite Bobby's opposition. The two men were not to comprise a mutual admiration society from that point on, though.

Jack Kennedy sometimes found himself apologizing for his younger brother's behavior during the campaign against Richard Nixon. "I don't think he's as patient as I am," he said at one point. "But he's overtired." Bobby Kennedy had every reason to be overtired. Whatever decisions did not absolutely have to be made by Jack were made by Bobby. "That was the big difference between our campaign last fall and Adlai Stevenson's in 1956," John Kennedy was to say when it was all over. "I didn't have to worry about anything except what I was going to say. . . ."

John Fitzgerald Kennedy was elected to the Presidency of the United States by the narrowest of margins. An exhausted Bobby sat up until dawn watching the returns from the West Coast. He didn't sleep until he was certain he had won.

Shortly after J.F.K.'s election to the Presidency, the Kennedy clan posed happily at Hyannis Port. Seated (left to right) are Eunice Shriver, Rose, Joseph, Jacque-

line, and Edward. Behind them are Ethel, Stephen and Jean Smith, the President-elect, Robert, Patricia Lawford, Sargent Shriver, Joan Kennedy, and Peter Lawford.

Chapter 5

THE ASSISTANT PRESIDENT

We're going to do what we thought Eisenhower was going to do in 1952 and never did—bring in a new spirit to the Government. Not necessarily young men, but new men, who believe in a cause, who believe their jobs go on forever, not just from nine to five. It really makes a hell of a difference.
—ROBERT F. KENNEDY

A President of the United States is one man, but a Presidency is myriad men. Now, with the victory parties out of the way, a tough job lay immediately ahead; a job that had to be done fast—and superlatively well. The men on whom the incoming administration would depend for its effectiveness had to be chosen. (Earlier, John Kennedy had said: "If I am elected, I don't want to wake up on the morning of November 9 and have to ask myself, 'What in the world do I do now?' ") Much of the responsibility for the choices to be made was delegated to Bobby Kennedy by a President-elect who exclaimed: "People, people, people! I don't know any people. I only know voters. How am I going to fill these 1200 jobs?"

One person John Kennedy *did* know was his

brother Robert, and one of those twelve hundred jobs to be filled was the attorney-generalship. Joe Kennedy, Sr. wanted Bobby to be named to the post, and when it was turned down by both Adlai Stevenson (who was not interested) and Abraham Ribicoff (who foresaw an awkward situation for John Kennedy if, in Arthur Schlesinger's words, "A Jewish Attorney General were putting Negro children in white schools in the South"), Bobby was approached. To say that he did not react with enthusiasm would be a massive understatement. For one thing, he had tired of "chasing people" during five years with the Rackets Committee; for another, he feared that enforcement of civil rights laws by a Kennedy would be all the more damaging to his brother's already minimal popularity in the South; finally, Bobby feared that such an appointment would leave the Kennedys wide open to charges of nepotism. ("Nepotism, my foot!" was Old Joe's reaction. "Why would anyone think that Bobby needs a job?") Joseph Kennedy, Sr. constituted minority opinion virtually in its entirety; the overwhelming consensus among Kennedy advisers was that Bobby should neither be offered the post nor accept it if it was offered. When the offer came, it came in the form of a presidential command. Bobby reluctantly obeyed. Asked how he would announce the appointment, John Kennedy replied: "Well, I think I'll open the front door of the Georgetown house some morning about 2 A.M., look up and down the street, and if there's no one there, I'll whisper, 'It's Bobby.' "

On December 16, 1960, on the steps of his home in Georgetown, President-elect Kennedy announced that his brother Robert would serve as Attorney General. A chorus of protest arose, but J.F.K. was adamant about having Bobby in his Cabinet. "I see nothing wrong," he quipped, "with giving Robert some legal experience as Attorney General before he goes out to practice law."

Bobby lost no time in reorganizing his department. Typically, one of his first choices was a former all-American football player, Byron ("Whizzer") White, whom he named as Deputy Attorney General. Archibald Cox of the Harvard Law School was appointed Solicitor General, and Burke Marshall, a onetime editor of the *Yale Law Journal,* was named to head the department's Civil Rights Division.

The responsibilities of an attorney general are many and varied, but it looked for a time as though Bobby Kennedy considered the post chiefly as a superior vantage point from which to attack his old bête noire, organized crime, and it seemed that the dignity of the Cabinet office might be tarnished somewhat by the pugnacity of its occupant. "I walk into Kennedy's office," reported a non-Harvard man named Joey Gallo, "and he gets mad at me. He says, 'So you're Joey Gallo, the jukebox king. You don't look so tough. I'd like to fight you myself.' I hadda tell him I don't fight."

At his first news conference, in April, Bobby announced an eight-point legislative program aimed, predictably enough, at organized crime and racketeering, and including a sweeping proposal to stop illegal interstate traffic in liquor and narcotics and to curb gambling, prostitution, bribery, and extortion. The proposed legislation, he announced, would drastically inconvenience "the bankrollers and kingpins of the rackets [who] live luxurious, apparently respectable lives in one state but return periodically to another state to collect from the

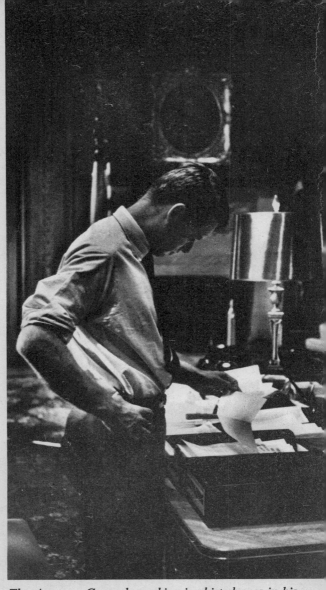

The Attorney General, working in shirt sleeves in his office, was photographed by Henri Cartiér-Bresson.

rackets they run by remote control." He then incurred the considerable displeasure of American businessmen by more or less lumping them together with the hoods with whom he seemed to be perpetually concerned. "We intend," he stated, "to take action not only against companies but also against those officials who we find to be responsible for price-fixing activities." Word was soon bruited about that the New Frontier was antibusiness, a charge that Bobby denied with little effect.

Nor had the Attorney General forgotten that he had an old score to settle. Indeed, even during the 1960 campaign, Jack had told a Salt Lake City audience that in his judgment, "an effective Attorney General with the present laws that we now have on the books can remove Mr. Hoffa from office. And I can assure you that both my brother and myself share a very deep conviction on the subject of Mr. Hoffa."

Soon after his appointment, Bobby set up a fifteen-man team, ostensibly to investigate racketeering in general in labor and management. For those less inclined to mince words, the group was immediately dubbed the "Get Hoffa Squad." By October, Hoffa had been indicted for the misuse of half a million dollars of Teamsters' money, and seven months later he was indicted again for allegedly accepting a million-dollar protection payoff. The fight was on again. Hoffa, supremely confident of winning, remarked: "If this kid don't get away from this crusade, he's going to crack up." The fight was to drag on for almost two more years.

Bobby was coming on, quite literally, like Gang-busters, but to many his concept of Justice Department priorities seemed more appropriate to the needs of the nineteen-thirties than to those of the sixties.

Then, both Robert and John Kennedy seemed to wake up to an awareness of the mounting seriousness of racial inequality. Bobby admitted with admirable candor that he had been slow to take up the Negro cause. "I won't say I stayed awake nights worrying about civil rights before I became Attorney General," he confessed, and his dilatory approach to the problem is understandable enough in the light of his almost total lack of prior exposure to it. To his great credit it can be said that when his awareness of Negro oppression was aroused, he neither hesitated nor at any time faltered in his determination to secure Negro rights. (Earlier, during John Kennedy's presidential campaign, Bobby had intervened on behalf of Dr. Martin Luther King, Jr. when the Negro leader had been jailed in Georgia—a gesture that was never to be forgotten by black America.)

In his blunt fashion, Bobby made the first formal declaration of his commitment to the Negro cause before a Southern audience. On May 6, 1961, at the University of Georgia Law School, he said: "I must tell you candidly what our policies are going to be in the field of civil rights. . . ." He then informed his listeners that whatever *their* sentiments regarding desegregation might be, *he* was going to enforce the law. He went on to admit that the record of his own department was somewhat tarnished, and that "very few Negroes were employed [there] above a custodial level." He had increased the number of Negro lawyers in the Justice Department from ten to fifty.

Two weeks later, the South provided the new Attorney General with the first chance to back his pledge with action when violence erupted in Montgomery, Alabama, as a Northern group of integrated Freedom Riders were met forcefully by local whites. Protection provided by the state turned out to be altogether inadequate. Bloody riots broke out and Bobby acted fast. Six hundred federal marshals were dispatched to Montgomery. One of their functions was to interpose themselves between the angry white mobs and Dr. King, who had arrived in town to conduct a prayer meeting. Eventually, the governor called his own National Guard in to quell the disturbances. Dr. King complained at the time that the federal forces were inadequate. As usual, Kennedy minced no words. "Doctor," he said, "if it wasn't for the U.S. marshals you'd be as dead as Kelsey's cow right now!" The two remained close until the day in April, 1968, when there were no federal marshals on hand to put themselves between King and the forces of violence.

Not all of the Justice Department's work in the South during Bobby's tenure was quite so spectacular, but it was nonetheless effective. Some quiet arm-twisting on the part of Burke Marshall and John Seigenthaler (a special assistant to Kennedy), who had toured the Southern states that spring, re-

During a trip around the world in 1962, Bobby and his wife visited Bali in Indonesia (above). In Tokyo (above right), they dined with Japan's Foreign Minister Zentaro Kosak, American Ambassador Edwin O. Reischauer, and geisha girls. Later, in Berlin, Bobby stood at Checkpoint Charlie and waved at East German guards.

sulted in the peaceable desegregation of schools in Atlanta, New Orleans, Memphis, and Dallas in the fall of 1961.

A year later, fireworks again erupted. The University of Mississippi, "Ole Miss," had been a citadel of racial purity since its opening in 1844. In January, 1961, a Negro named James Meredith had attempted the unthinkable: enrollment at the university. He had been turned down and had appealed to the United States Fifth Circuit Court. In June, 1962, the court had found that he had been illegally deprived of his rights, and the decision was upheld by the Supreme Court. In Mississippi, Governor Ross Barnett defied the highest judicial body in the land by declaring that Mississippians would "not surrender to the evil and illegal forces of tyranny." Kennedy stood firm, but offered Barnett a face-saving expedient. Barnett accepted the deal, then reneged. The deal was reoffered, reaccepted, and then reneged on again. The Attorney General acted. On September 30, 1962, federal marshals escorted Meredith into a dormitory on the Oxford campus. As evening approached, rioting broke out. Eventually, contingents of the United States Army were required to put down the disturbances. The law had been enforced.

When Martin Luther King returned to Alabama (in April, 1963) and began a series of sit-ins and marches, the Birmingham police commissioner, Eugene ("Bull") Connor, treated King's followers to a demonstration of Southern hospitality that included the use of fire hoses, German shepherds, and electric cattle prods. Burke Marshall was dispatched to the riot-torn city at Kennedy's order. On May 10, he announced a "settlement" with local officials. While it did not achieve complete equality for the Birmingham Negro, it did bring about an uneasy desegregation of some public accommodations, and an agreement for nondiscriminatory hiring by the city's bigger employers. Considering the viciousness of the initial opposition, it was a major accomplishment for the Attorney General.

Other events, of course, were taking place while all this was going on, some of them of crucial importance. Hardly had the New Frontier been organized, when the Kennedy administration received the first—and worst—blow to its prestige. The ill-advised Bay of Pigs venture had backfired completely, and—indicative both of Bobby's growing stature and of the President's growing dependency on his younger brother—the Attorney General was summoned to help pick up the pieces. There were not many pieces left to be picked up, but it was generally agreed that he did a superlative job of ascertaining why things had gone wrong. He also demonstrated just how tough he could be with anyone whose loyalty to his brother was less than complete. "So you advised against this operation," he reportedly told Undersecretary of State Chester Bowles. "Well, as of now, you were all for it."

Bobby Kennedy's temper was still an unpredictable quantity, and his penchant for caustic excoriation of those who opposed him had undergone no diminishment, but he *was* growing up fast and

A portrait of grief: Robert, Jacqueline, and Edward Kennedy at the funeral of the assassinated John Kennedy

increasingly displayed (in Hemingway's phrase) grace under pressure. His role in the Cuban Missile Crisis, it was later agreed, was of crucial importance, and when the affair entered its most critical phase, his was the most audible voice of reason. At one point a hastily summoned Executive Committee, composed of members of the National Security Council, was seriously considering ordering a surprise air strike on Cuba, regardless of the awesome consequences such a strike might bring about. The Attorney General called it "another Pearl Harbor in reverse," and the idea was abandoned. Bobby strongly backed Secretary of Defense Robert McNamara's suggestion that a blockade be established around the island, the plan that was adopted. On October 26, 1962, the almost unbearable tension that had built up while the world teetered on the brink of total nuclear war was momentarily eased. In a secret letter to the President, Premier Khrushchev had offered a peaceful settlement that included accession to the major American demand—withdrawal of all missiles from Cuban sites. Then, a second letter, following almost immediately, attached the proviso that United States missiles be removed from Turkey. It was Bobby who suggested that the President ignore the second letter and answer the first in a conciliatory tone. By October 28, the Russians began dismantling their Cuban missile installations, and the world, thanks to "a brash young brat who thinks he can ride his brother's coattails," breathed easier.

Despite the tensions and despite the crises; despite a seemingly irreducible sea of troubles at home and abroad, the years of John F. Kennedy's administration were good years, and nobody was enjoying them more than Robert Kennedy, who drove himself relentlessly and still found time to play. Problems notwithstanding, Washington was a joyous place, and Washingtonians—and most Americans—were imbued with a new sense of purpose. A young, handsome, and dynamic President was approaching his peak and the nation looked forward with a new expectancy to each passing day. And then, on a bright November day in 1963, it all came crashing down.

Chapter 6

OFF AND RUNNING

Jack had traveled a great deal in the realms of doubt, whereas Bobby has never explored those regions yet.
— JEAN KENNEDY SMITH

Certainty is the privilege of the immature; doubt and growth go hand in hand. For years people had been saying that Robert Kennedy lived in a black-and-white world; that for him there was right and there was wrong, with no shadings of difference in between; that his vocabulary admitted only "yes" and "no," with the possibility of a following "if" precluded.

Of course, Bobby was not quite that simplistic. He was a highly intelligent man, with a mind analytical enough to cut through complexities to the essence of a problem. Still, there was a measure of truth in the commonly held notion of how he viewed the world—at least until that point where he really began to shoulder some of the responsibilities of the world. The Bobby Kennedy of the Cuban Missile

Crisis was a different Bobby Kennedy from the "brat" that Jimmy Hoffa had known—just as John Kennedy, living with the responsibilities of power, was not the "whippersnapper" that Dwight Eisenhower had previously taken him to be. And yet, by late 1963, Bobby Kennedy had not very thoroughly explored the regions of doubt. The brashness and the cockiness were tempered, perhaps, but nothing had occurred in the course of his thirty-eight years to cause him deeply to search his soul.

The awful occurrence of November 22, 1963, changed all that.

In the immediate aftermath of his brother's assassination, Bobby Kennedy did what had to be done. Then, with his family duties discharged, he began a long journey through the regions of doubt—and of despair. The body of a vital, dynamic young man lay in Arlington Cemetery. And at nearby Hickory Hill a younger and even more dynamic man was sinking into a profound lethargy. It was a nearly complete withdrawal from life, almost as though he were trying to replace his brother in the grave. Even the words he had waited longest to hear failed to rouse him: the news that Jimmy Hoffa had at last been convicted—some three months after the assassination—was to elicit from him only an abstracted "Nice work." "If there ever was a lost soul at that time," a member of the family said later, "it was Bobby." When he found his way again, he was in every way an older man.

It was Lyndon Baines Johnson who took the first step in leading him out of the woods. There had been no love lost between the two men since their political paths had first crossed in 1960, and their antagonism had in no way been alleviated by the events that immediately followed the assassination. Bobby had bitterly resented what he took to be a too quick take-over by Johnson, and Johnson's opinion of him, not very high in the best of circumstances, was lowered considerably by what *he* considered a deliberate attempt to sabotage his first Cabinet meeting (reluctant to attend it at all, Bobby had shown up late). In January, however, Johnson asked Bobby to undertake a delicate mission to the Far East, where President Sukarno of Indonesia was threatening the continued existence of the newly created Federation of Malaysia. Kennedy had met with Sukarno in Indonesia on an earlier mission in 1962; this time, their initial talks were held in Tokyo.

Diplomatically, the meetings were of dubious value. After several discussions with Kennedy, Sukarno agreed to a cease-fire, but soon resumed exhorting his country to "crush Malaysia." The spiritual rewards of the trip, though, were of incalculable value to Bobby. On a previous trip to Japan, he had been all but hooted off the stage when he addressed the anti-American students of Waseda University; now he was given an equally tumultuous reception— but a friendly one. The death of his brother, Robert Kennedy realized, had *not* ended the world, but instead seemed to have given it a new sense of purpose. "If President Kennedy's life and death are to mean anything," Bobby told his audience, "we

Bobby Kennedy visits his brother's grave on January 20, 1965, Lyndon Baines Johnson's Inauguration Day.

young people must work harder for a better life for all the people of the world." He himself was no longer one of the "young people." (As a Waseda professor remarked, "Two years ago Kennedy looked boyish and full of go. Today he looks older, far more mature and full of signs of deepening wisdom.") He was, however, ready to go back to work.

The question was: What work? He had become disenchanted with the attorney-generalship; the job was not what it had been during his brother's administration, when he had been the nation's number 2 man (or, as some insiders had it, "number 1½"). Friends were urging him to run for a Senate seat in New York or for the governorship of Massachusetts. At one point he impulsively requested the ambassadorship to Vietnam, but was turned down by President Johnson on the grounds that the risk of losing another Kennedy was too great. Finally, there was the possibility of the second spot on the national ticket in 1964, which, as Kennedy continued to consider the various possibilities, became increasingly attractive. It had its drawbacks, of course ("There isn't anything you can do in the Vice-Presidency . . . not one damn thing . . . that you are not told to do"), not the least of which was that it required direct subservience to a man whom he resented and who, he had implied, was reducing the Presidency from "excellence" to "mediocrity." The great virtue of the Vice-Presidency, however, was that it would put him in direct line for the succession when Johnson left the White House. Kennedy let it be known that he would not turn down the

Rejected as a vice-presidential candidate by Lyndon Johnson in 1964, Kennedy opposed Kenneth Keating in New York's senatorial election. Although he was denounced as a "carpetbagger," he drew crowds during the campaign (above.) Below, he wears a skullcap in a synagogue in an effort to win votes.

chance to be President Johnson's running mate.

With Barry Goldwater fast shaping up as his November opponent, Johnson hardly needed the glamour of a Kennedy on the ticket to win. There was no other reason for Johnson to want Bobby as his Vice-President—and there was a plethora of reasons for not wanting him. On July 29, 1964, Kennedy was invited to Johnson's office and informed that the President did not want him. To avoid embarrassment, Johnson publicly announced that he deemed it advisable to exclude all Cabinet members from consideration as vice-presidential candidates. In a speech a few days later, Bobby said he was sorry to have taken "so many nice fellows over the side with me."

The "R.F.K.-L.B.J. feud" was advancing apace. Johnson supporters cut all pictures of Bobby out of a film biography of John F. Kennedy that was to be shown at the Democratic National Convention. Bobby *was* allowed to make an introductory speech before the film's showing, however, and the reception he was given by the delegates was, as William Shannon put it in *The Heir Apparent,* "an extraordinary outburst of grief, love, and frustration." When the demonstration finally subsided, Kennedy delivered a brief address highlighted by a passage from *Romeo and Juliet*:

"When he shall die
Take him and cut him out in little stars,
And he will make the face of heaven so fine
That all the world will be in love with night
And pay no worship to the garish sun."

The President, if he was listening, could not have missed the allusion in the last line.

Bobby Kennedy's choices had narrowed. There were useful jobs he could do in Washington, but there were none available that would in any way advance his claim as the heir apparent. Of the remaining possibilities, a gubernatorial race in Massachusetts was ruled out as a probable diluent of Senator Ted Kennedy's power in the state. There remained the state of New York, and a Senate seat held by a Republican, Kenneth Keating. New York had its complications, not the least of which was Kennedy's nonresidence, a condition that would leave him open to charges of "carpetbagging."

After weighing the pros and cons of the matter, Bobby decided to run. Some thought that in effect he was running not for the Senate but for the Presidency of the United States in 1968; somewhere along the line, in the midst of his broodings on the future and what it held in store, he seemed to have concluded that '68 might be both the earliest and latest year in which to try for the goal he had been pointed at from birth. He would then be only forty-two, true, but his brother had been only a year older in 1960, and as a member of a singularly star-crossed family, he felt that "long-range plans don't make much sense. . . . Who knows whether any of us will even be alive then?" In any case, he secured the nomination as New York's Democratic candidate for the Senate in early September, and then announced his resignation as Attorney General.

Despite the carpetbagging charges, the charges

When the Kennedys visited Ethiopia in 1966, Emperor Haile Selassie introduced them to a pet cheetah and convinced Ethel that it was safe for her to pat its head.

The previous year, Bobby and Ethel had visited South America, where he demonstrated that the Kennedy charisma transcended language barriers. Right: Lima, Peru.

With Ethel and their children, the junior senator from New York watches the Super Bowl football game on TV.

that Bobby was capitalizing on his martyred brother's name, and the charges that he would, if elected, occupy himself more with the national build-up for a presidential race than with the less enthralling problems of his constituents, Bobby was obviously charming his way into the hearts of the voters. Moreover, he was not *just* charming them, but also convincing them that "strange as it may seem, I just want to be a good United States Senator." Some of Keating's followers, fearing that their candidate was running a losing race, went on the offensive. Charges of McCarthyism and anti-Semitism were leveled wildly at Bobby, and he was accused, as Attorney General, of having made "a deal with Nazis." The latter charge was based on his settlement of a long-drawn-out case concerning the General Aniline and Film Corporation, which had been seized as enemy property during World War II.

Kennedy turned back all charges convincingly, reminding voters angrily that "I lost a brother and a brother-in-law to the Nazis. I'm not making any deals with Nazis." On November 3, 1964, he won his first election. "We started something in 1960, and the vote today is an overwhelming mandate to continue," he told a cheering audience.

Robert Kennedy's Senate record was a lot better than many people thought it would be, and as *Life* noted, his first two years on Capitol Hill saw him "emerge gradually from [John F. Kennedy's] reflected glow into a clear and powerful identity of his own." It was not a sharpening or magnification of his earlier identity, either. He was still tough, but no longer "ruthless"; he was still confident, but no longer cocky. More important, he now seemed motivated not so much by the old need to win for himself as by the need to win for humanity.

During his freshman year in the Senate, he concentrated on the problems of the minority groups and the poor of New York State. With Republican Senator Jacob Javits, for example, he cosponsored an amendment to allow one hundred thousand non-English-speaking Puerto Ricans to exercise their franchise. The following year, he called attention to the explosive situation in the Bedford-Stuyvesant area of Brooklyn, one of the nation's largest black ghettos, and triggered implementation of a program designed to revitalize the area and to redevelop it substantially. In contrast to many of his colleagues, whose interests seemed to lie wherever the money and the power were, he made the ghetto areas his "special constituencies," according to the *Times,* and those constituencies in turn "considered him their special Senator."

Kennedy's concern for these constituents notwithstanding, his major concern was Vietnam, and this was to convert the R.F.K.-L.B.J. feud into a complete and irrevocable rupture. Earlier, he had supported administration policy in Vietnam, but as the months dragged on and casualty figures mounted, and as the American commitment began to seem more the product of compulsion than of conviction, he reversed his stand and started to press for a negotiated settlement. He also questioned the accuracy of Defense Department estimates of enemy strength, and foresaw an exercise in waste and futility that "promises only years and decades of further draining conflict . . . [which] could lead us only to national tragedy." "If you keep talking like this," President Johnson scolded him, "you won't have a political future in this country within six months." Kennedy later denied that he had replied to Johnson profanely, but the rift was final and complete.

He continued to speak out against the war and to urge a halt to the bombing of North Vietnam. "It should be clear by now," he said on March 2, 1967, "that the bombing of the North cannot bring an end to the war in the South; rather that it may well be prolonging the war. . . . It is not weakness for this great nation to take a generous step toward ending the war. It is not bravery to refuse an act which may save thousands of lives with little risk to ourselves. Can anyone believe this nation, with all its fantastic power and resources, will be endangered by a wise and magnanimous action toward a difficult but small adversary? Not escalation, but an effort to achieve negotiation, now opens the most hopeful prospect to peace."

Robert Kennedy could still behave emotionally and with a distorted sense of family loyalty (as the notorious "Battle of the Book"—in which he gave William Manchester, author of *The Death of a President*, a very hard time indeed—made clear), but on the whole he had changed. "When I first met him," Theodore Sorensen remarked, ". . . I would not have voted for him for anything. He was much more cocky, militant, negative, narrow, closer to his father in thinking than to his brother. Today I have no serious doubts about him. . . . I would vote for him for anything."

To those closest to him as the first stirrings of the presidential campaign of 1968 were felt, his concern over Vietnam, poverty, racial inequality, and the spread of violence seemed not a mere political "handle" but something far deeper and more abiding. He was still to plunge into a political contest zestfully, but he was nonetheless in a process of metamorphosis: he was changing from politician to statesman.

He was coming of age.

Hard-fought touch football games, in which ladies took part, were a frequent occurrence at Kennedy's home.

Chapter 7

THE RUN FOR THE MONEY

The trouble with this campaign is that the candidate doesn't have a Robert Kennedy working for him.
—A DEMOCRATIC NATIONAL COMMITTEEWOMAN

Almost from the moment that John Kennedy received word of his brother Joe's death in 1944, it was a foregone conclusion that he would one day make a bid for the Presidency. And almost from the moment of *his* death in 1963, it was generally considered inevitable that Robert Kennedy would one day in the not too distant future make a bid of his own.

There were other factors besides the family line of succession. As Margaret Laing noted in *The Next Kennedy,* Bobby had "no choice but to try to be President, because that is in clear and simple terms a way of winning. . . ." More explicitly, it was for Bobby—the most competitive Kennedy of them all —the *only* way of winning. The Presidency is, in John Kennedy's celebrated phrase, "where the power is"; it is the highest political post available, and to settle for any post beneath the highest would be, by Old Joe Kennedy's well-absorbed standards, settling for a second choice. That the Kennedys themselves were quite well aware of this was made absolutely clear by the inscription on a cigarette case presented to Bobby by the President-elect in 1960: "When I'm through, how about you?" By 1967, there was hardly an adult in the country who did not assume that Bobby Kennedy would eventually go after the presidential nomination. The only question was when.

As the war dragged on in Vietnam, unrest increased at home, and Lyndon Johnson's popularity continued to decline. Senator Kennedy's admirers began besieging him with pleas to run. As one magazine writer observed, "Hardly a day passed that somebody didn't chide him, 'Why don't you take on Lyndon Johnson?' It became a part of life, like breathing or touch football. No man ever had more offers to hold his coat while he got out there and mixed it with Big Sonny [a reference to prize fighter Sonny Liston]."

In characteristic fashion, Bobby submitted the question of running against Johnson for the nomination to intensive analysis at the beginning of 1968. He had the advice of several members of the New Frontier. Their conclusion—and his own—was that the incumbent President was unbeatable, barring an absolutely unforeseen eventuality. Bobby's decision was to wait until 1972.

Then, on March 12, the absolutely unforeseen

Ethel smiles at the antics of two of her children as Bobby announces that he will run for the Presidency.

eventuality came to pass: Senator Eugene McCarthy of Minnesota ran up over 42 per cent of the vote in the New Hampshire primary, leaving a badly damaged Lyndon Johnson wondering what had hit him. McCarthy and his "Children's Crusade" of underage volunteers had generally been written off as a political joke; if a joke was all it took to make an "unbeatable" candidate look like the victim of a sandbagging, it was obvious that Robert Kennedy's position could stand some reassessment. Four days later, while McCarthy was still enjoying the first flush of success and the President's supporters were still reeling, Robert F. Kennedy moved to the podium in the Senate caucus room and stated what was by then blindingly obvious: "These are not ordinary times and this is not an ordinary election." The inevitable had occurred; Bobby Kennedy was running for the Presidency of the United States.

Robert Kennedy's entry into the race was bound to incur the wrath not only of the Kennedy-haters, but also of the McCarthy supporters, who naturally resented his getting into the act after *their* hero had punctured the myth of Johnson's invulnerability. Nor, needless to say, did it further endear him to Lyndon Johnson (who had spurned Kennedy's offer to stay out of the race provided he, the President, would publicly announce his intention of reevaluating the United States' role in Vietnam). Finally, it earned him the animosity of a good many Democrats who thought he was splitting the party.

Kennedy supporters maintained that their man had already decided to announce his candidacy

A few weeks before his death, R.F.K. and Ethel posed for this picture with nine of their ten children. From

left to right are Matthew, Christopher, Kerry, Michael, Courtney, David, Robert, Joseph, and Kathleen.

before the New Hampshire upset, but feared that to do so would hurt the peace movement by fragmenting any force it might show in the balloting. They discounted the charge that he had lacked the courage to tackle Johnson earlier, maintaining that to have done so would have seemed the result of a vendetta, and not of a deep disagreement on the issues. Finally, they claimed somewhat abstrusely that it was Nelson Rockefeller's meager write-in vote in New Hampshire, not Johnson's poor showing, that had convinced Kennedy he could win.

Then, while the pros and cons of the Kennedy candidacy were still being debated, the biggest bombshell of them all exploded: on March 31, Lyndon Baines Johnson announced to a stunned nation that he would not run for re-election. The announcement left the two surviving candidates fundamentally in agreement and temporarily deprived of an opponent; the idea all along had been that neither of them could really beat Johnson flat out, but that together they might nail down enough delegate strength to prevent a first-ballot renomination for the President. Without that first-ballot triumph, it was thought, Johnson's own delegate strength would quickly evaporate.

The opponent turned up the next month, when, after considerable procrastination, Vice-President Humphrey threw *his* hat into the ring.

As the contest got under way, Robert Kennedy had a number of things going for him. For one, the magic of his name, and for another, the desire of a fair share of the electorate for a "return to

Camelot." He also had a crack staff, made up in large part of former New Frontiersmen, and he had abundant financial resources. Additionally, he could count on the Negro vote, the votes of other minority groups, and the votes of the poor. Less tangibly, he had a tremendous amount of charisma. Finally, he was not the brash young man he had been in 1960. A good deal of mellowing had taken place in the intervening eight years, and at times he bore a startling resemblance in looks and manner to his martyred brother.

He could not, of course, avoid the resemblance, but in contrast to his campaign for the Senate, he seemed consciously to avoid trading on John Kennedy's name or accomplishments. "The policies of the thirties," he announced, "were not adequate for the sixties, and the policies of the early sixties are not adequate to meet the problems of the seventies and eighties."

Kennedy's first test came with the Indiana primary of May 7. He won it handily after an intensive campaign, garnering 42 per cent of the vote to 31 per cent for Governor Roger Branigin, Humphrey's stand-in, and an unimpressive 27 per cent for McCarthy, who maintained, nevertheless, that he had not been defeated. "I was always taught that it is much better to win," Old Joe Kennedy's son retorted. "I learned that when I was about two." The campaign moved on to Nebraska, and there, in a predominantly rural state with a 2 per cent Negro population, Kennedy scored heavily, taking just over half the vote to McCarthy's 31 per cent. Hubert

Humphrey was still a force to be reckoned with, but as far as a McCarthy threat was concerned, the campaign looked like a cakewalk. Kennedy's staff and followers were jubilant. There had been a kind of jubilation about the whole campaign from its inception, and it seemed to be largely a matter of closeness to Bobby. Repeatedly, veteran newsmen remarked on the peculiarly self-contained atmosphere of the Kennedy group; of how it seemed to constitute an almost perfect little world of its own—a hectic sort of world perhaps, but one in which an underlying harmony reigned. Strangely enough, this man who for so long had been characterized as "cold" and "ruthless" and a master of hatred seemed capable now of giving and inspiring a great deal of something very much like love. The abstracted glance and perfunctory handshake had been replaced by a need for real, indeed physical, contact with people. And the need was unmistakably genuine. As Hays Gorey commented in *Time,* "No one who has seen Kennedy on the Indian reservations of Arizona or Idaho, no one who has seen him in the stinking hovels of Appalachia, no one who has seen him take the hand of a starving Negro child in the Mississippi Delta, accuses him of acting. Neither he nor any other politician could be that good an actor."

Joyously, the Kennedy campaign headed for California, and for the last and biggest primary of them all. There would be a prior test in Oregon along the way, but that hardly seemed to matter any more. Two weeks later, the Kennedy campaign *was* in

A typical Kennedy scene: walking with admirers during a tour of Harlem, the nation's largest black community

California—and Kennedy was in trouble. Beaten by Eugene McCarthy in the Oregon primary, he had exactly no time in which to find a winning formula for the final contest—and six days in which to apply it. A campaign that hitherto had been notable for its gaiety and *esprit de corps* had suddenly turned into something resembling a dispirited rout.

All the winning formulas had been used in Oregon, but they somehow hadn't worked. In an overwhelmingly white state, Kennedy had based too much of his pitch on the plight of the Negro. In one of the Union's more prosperous states, he had hammered away at poverty. Moreover, he had almost dared the electorate to slap him down by telling them he would no longer be a "viable candidate" without their support, and had antagonized a fair number of voters by speaking too often of the specifics of regions no outsider could have been expected to know; to many Oregonians that had looked too much like a slick Eastern research job (which it was), and was resented. Furthermore, he had run largely on his personality, feeding wisecracks instead of ideas to audiences in a state that demands serious discussion of issues. Finally, Kennedy had all but ignored McCarthy (who had offered to debate with him) and had concentrated his fire on Hubert Humphrey—who didn't happen to be on the Oregon ballot.

On Wednesday, May 29, Kennedy had vowed to withdraw from the race if he were beaten again the following Tuesday in California. Actually, the announcement was supererogatory, for a defeat in

California would for all practical purposes have *knocked* him out of the race; about all it accomplished was to provide McCarthy with an excuse for dredging up a not altogether unfounded charge that had haunted Kennedy since childhood: that he was a poor loser. Kennedy badly needed to regroup his forces and he knew it. "I'm not the same candidate I was before Oregon," he acknowledged. Then, he couldn't resist wisecracking again (although somewhat ruefully) and announced that "after last night in Oregon I'm going to call Los Angeles Resurrection City"—a remark that was to take on a heartbreaking poignancy a few days later.

That same Wednesday, a relaxed, smiling Eugene McCarthy left Oregon with the announcement that he expected to win in the neighboring state. While the announcement was predictable enough, McCarthy's real strength in California was not; he had already pulled off a couple of political miracles during the campaign, not the least of which was his victory of the night before, and he seemed to be leading a charmed life. The depression of the Kennedy forces would have been understandable enough even without the annoyances to come. Among other things, the Oregon defeat had been the first undergone by any member of the present Kennedy generation in twenty-seven primary and general-election campaigns.

As one reporter assessing the situation put it, "All that stardust" had "turned to dandruff." It was a crack Bobby Kennedy himself might have got off in a less despondent moment. Now, he wanly remarked that he and McCarthy "can both take some satisfaction from the overwhelming support for a change the voters have registered."

On Thursday in California, the mood brightened. Kennedy had agreed to meet McCarthy in a nationally televised debate, and his supporters, perhaps remembering the Nixon-J.F.K. debates of 1960 and possibly expecting history to repeat, were full of confidence. As one member of the press corps put it, life on the Kennedy campaign train "seemed like old times." Still, there were some misgivings among the more analytically minded; for Kennedy to accept McCarthy's challenge now, after turning it down earlier, seemed a dangerous admission that McCarthy was no patsy.

Kennedy was in San Francisco the next morning. The weather was bright and so was his mood. "I'm delighted to be here in California," he told a conservative audience at the Commonwealth Club. "I came here from Nebraska." The response was enthusiastic. In Oregon, Kennedy had been completely at sea ("How do you get a handle on a state like this?" a campaign strategist wailed). His audiences had been unresponsive enough to impel him to wish aloud for at least a few catcalls. Now, in California, he could again capitalize on his personality. He told his Commonwealth Club audience that he had ridden a cable car that morning and "was enjoying it immensely until John Glenn turned to me and said, 'I'm scared.' "

On Saturday, June 1, three days before the primary, Kennedy remained in San Francisco, taking it relatively easy and enjoying the sunshine on Fisherman's Wharf. That evening was the evening of the debate, which turned out to be rather inconclusive. But the mood was still good.

The mood held through Sunday, with Kennedy jokingly asking a young woman reporter who she thought looked "more presidential," himself or McCarthy, and telling his wife, Ethel, to try to keep her California cities straight (she had mistaken Anaheim for Los Angeles at one point). Both Kennedys were delighted when six of their children boarded their plane at Anaheim. The good mood held.

Monday, the final day of the California campaign, was different. The campaign had been growing increasingly vituperative as it came down to the wire, everyone was jittery, and Kennedy was exhausted. Then, after a hurried breakfast and a flight to San Francisco, the firecracker incident occurred. Ethel Kennedy grabbed her husband and pulled him down. In Long Beach, someone ended a good speech on a ghastly note by calling out: "Who killed your brother?" Then Kennedy got sick in San Diego. The mood had turned sour.

Bobby and Ethel, about to board their campaign plane

Chapter 8

SO THIS IS IT

Men are not made for safe havens.
—EDITH HAMILTON

To say that the dispirited mood of the day before had been broken would be a prodigious understatement. Pandemonium reigned in the Embassy ballroom as the candidate, flashing his toothy grin, made for a short flight of portable stairs. He had planned to go directly from the ballroom to The Factory, a chic Los Angeles discotheque that had been commandeered for the postelection whoop-up, but in the very last moments of his victory speech, aides had agreed to a brief conference with newsmen in the press room. Kennedy seemed confused for a moment about which way to turn. The crowd was surging toward the rostrum, and for once, he decided to avoid contact with the people and turned for a rear passageway leading, through a kitchen corridor, to the Colonial Room, where the press

In May, 1965, Senator Kennedy testified before the Senate Juvenile Delinquency Subcommittee to urge legislation curbing mail-order sale of guns. Prompt action, he said, "would save hundreds of lives in this country and spare thousands of families all across this land the grief and heartbreak that may come from the loss of a husband, a son, a brother. . . ." At top left is a duplicate of the rifle used to kill John F. Kennedy.

corps was assembled. Bill Barry, a bodyguard, tried to dissuade him, somehow not liking the idea, but Kennedy said, "It's all right," and slipped through a curtain behind the speaker's platform.

A number of those invited to the Factory party had started for the ballroom's main door, but then, seeing Bobby change course, they doubled back and jockeyed for position closer to him. The heat was terrific, and so was the crush. Faces, many of them familiar, flashed by, strangely lurid in the glare of the TV floodlights. (On the East Coast, many of those diehards who had stayed up to watch the victor claim his spoils were wearily turning off their sets. The speech had been a happy, formless mixture of family jokes and political credo.)

Bobby entered the kitchen, surrounded by a tumultuous, jostling mob. Roosevelt Grier, the huge football player, and the tall, lanky writer George Plimpton were easily discernible above a sea of heads. Rafer Johnson, the other Negro athlete who had accompanied the candidate through California, was there, too, as were Jesse Unruh, Bobby's state campaign manager, and a host of other aides, admirers, intimates, hangers-on, hotel employees, and total strangers. A teen-ager named Lisa Urso squeezed her way through the crush and maneuvered her way in front of Kennedy, only to be pushed aside by the crowd.

There were more hands to be shaken, and the grinning faces of the kitchen staff, lined up behind the steam tables, to be grinned at. Kennedy reached for an outstretched hand, turning at the same time to see if his wife, Ethel, was still with him. Then a sharp crack, followed by a series of small explosions, froze the grins on the faces nearest the candidate. Kennedy's right hand went to the back of his head. An instant later he was on the floor, face upward, his right arm outflung and rigid, the bloody fist clenched.

The crackle of gunfire seemed to go on forever; people seemed to be falling everywhere. At the core of the confusion, men were cursing, women screaming. Rosey Grier and Rafer Johnson had pounced on a small squirming figure in blue. Plimpton and Barry threw themselves onto the pileup. A Mutual Network broadcaster, Andrew West, was babbling almost incoherently into his tape recorder: "Senator Kennedy . . . Oh my God! Senator Kennedy has been shot—and another man, a Kennedy campaign manager—and possibly shot in the *head!* . . . Rafer Johnson has hold of a man who has apparently fired the shot. . . . He still has the gun! The gun is pointed at me right this moment! . . . Be very careful. Get the gun. Get the gun. Get the *gun!* Stay away from the guy! Stay away from the gun. His *hand* is frozen—Get his thumb! Get his THUMB! GET HIS THUMB, GET HIS THUMB, GET . . . HIS . . . THUMB! *Break* it if you have to. Get his thumb. Get away from the barrel. Get away from the *barrel,* man! Look out for the gun. . . ."

Others—everyone—were shouting at once: "Get a doctor! We need a doctor!" The cry "Oh no!" and cries of "Oh my God!" filled the kitchen corridor, then traveled out across the ballroom. And West's tape recorder whirred on: "That's it, Rafer, get it. Get the gun, Rafer. Okay. Now hold on to the gun. . . . They have the gun away from the man. In this . . . they've got the gun. I can't see the man. I can't see who it is. Senator Kennedy . . . has been shot. This is—This is—What is it? Wait a minute. Hold him! Hold him, HOLD HIM! We don't want another Oswald! Hold him, Rafer, we don't . . . want . . . another . . . OSWALD!"

Steve Smith, Kennedy's brother-in-law, was pleading with the crowd to clear the ballroom. Ethel Kennedy, pregnant with her eleventh child, was fighting her way to her husband's side in the kitchen. And then a scene of shattering poignancy was enacted: a youth was yelling something about "Kennedy," and Ethel was saying, "Don't talk that way about the senator." And then she was kneeling to kiss the cheek of the same young man, who had been shot and now lay groaning in a smear of blood.

It was now obvious that Robert Kennedy was gravely wounded. Someone held an ice pack to the back of his head, which was bleeding badly. A priest appeared from somewhere to administer last rites (the senator's shirt had been torn open and his hand clutched a rosary). The priest was shoved aside as someone screamed, "He doesn't need a priest, for God's sake, he needs a doctor!" The senator's head was pillowed on someone's crumpled jacket, and his kneeling wife was trying to fend off photographers with an outstretched arm. "Get them out!" she screamed. "Give him air!" "This is history, lady," a cameraman said, triggering a flashbulb.

*A few moments before he was shot, Kennedy made a
victory speech in the ballroom of his Los Angeles hotel.*

And in the midst of chaos, one man in the room seemed strangely at peace. "The lips were slightly parted," Hays Gorey of *Time* wrote later, "the lower one curled downwards, as it often was. Bobby seemed aware. There was no questioning in his expression. He didn't ask, 'What happened?' [He] seemed almost to say, 'So this is it.'"

Roosevelt Grier, defensive tackle for the Los Angeles Rams, is one of the most powerful men alive; Rafer Johnson is a superbly conditioned all-round athlete; George Plimpton (a superbly out-of-condition would-be athlete) is a sizable man; and so is Bill Barry. Yet, all four of them, plus a couple of hotel employees and a pair of Kennedy aides, were having trouble with the little man with the gun. He kept pumping shots into the crowd, until five persons besides Kennedy had been hit and all eight shells had been expended from his .22-caliber Iver-Johnson Cadet revolver. Finally, he was pinned, still squirming, to a serving counter. "Why did you do it?" Johnson screamed. "Why did you *do* it?" "I can explain," the little man replied. "Let me explain!"

A number of men had no intention of letting him explain, but Unruh kept bellowing, "I want him alive! I want him alive!"—echoing the thought already expressed by the broadcaster West: the nation could not afford another Oswald fiasco. Grier and Johnson literally had to drag several would-be lynchers off the man. Then the police arrived and the little man was taken away. He was hustled down a flight of stairs by a tight ring of cops, his feet barely meeting the steps, as cries of "Get the bastard!" filled the air. Kennedy still lay on the floor.

When Dr. Roland Dean reached Kennedy, about eleven minutes after the candidate had concluded his speech with the word "win," he found him conscious, and on the basis of a superficial examination, termed his condition "critical." But he seemed guardedly optimistic. There was little he or the two other doctors on the scene could do, however. Then finally, after twenty-three agonizingly slow minutes, an ambulance arrived at the hotel. As the senator was lifted, as gently as possible, onto a stretcher, he murmured, "No, no, don't."

At exactly twelve forty-eight, the stretcher was rolled into Central Receiving Hospital's Emergency Room No. 2, and the patient was prepared for heart-lung resuscitation. A doctor appeared, and after remarking, "the bullet hit the switchboard," got to work. At one point he slapped Kennedy's face repeatedly, while Ethel winced at each slap and implored him to stop. Oxygen was forced down the patient's throat; adrenalin, albumin, and a blood substitute were administered. Suddenly there were signs of life and Bobby began visibly to breathe again. Ethel Kennedy was allowed to listen to her husband's heartbeat through a stethoscope. Then it was decided to move him to the better-equipped Good Samaritan Hospital, four blocks away. A team of six neurosurgeons had begun to assemble there.

The horror was worse in its way than the first minutes after his brother's shooting. *That,* at least,

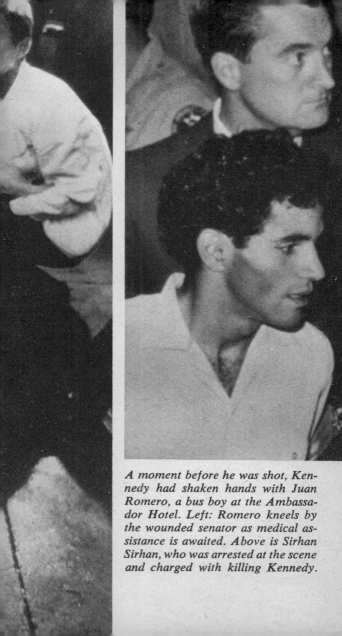

A moment before he was shot, Kennedy had shaken hands with Juan Romero, a bus boy at the Ambassador Hotel. Left: Romero kneels by the wounded senator as medical assistance is awaited. Above is Sirhan Sirhan, who was arrested at the scene and charged with killing Kennedy.

had come as a bolt from the blue, before people had begun talking of "the Kennedys and fate." *This* had been too consciously feared—almost expected—especially during the last few days. As one member of the press corps was to write: "There is grief. But more, there is a kind of weird acceptance."

Now, there were hopes and prayers, but a sickening, gut-wrenching finality hung over it all, as though some vengeful nemesis had singled out the Kennedys for early, violent death. (Richard Cardinal Cushing perhaps expressed it best when he said, with unpriestly despair: "We could continue our prayers that it would never happen again, but we did that before.")

At half past three (Washington time), President Johnson was roused by telephone, woke Lady Bird, and joined the vigil. All across the continent, telephones rang out a rude awakening for millions, summoning them to join the vigil. And a nation held its collective breath. Then, at 4:45 A.M. (Pacific time), Frank Mankiewicz, Robert Kennedy's press secretary, emerged from the hospital and climbed atop a police squad car. "I have a very short announcement to make," he began. "The doctors now say that the surgery will take another hour or perhaps two. . . ." The wait resumed.

Curiously, John F. Kennedy's widow got the news not from California, but from London. Her sister and brother-in-law wanted to know how Bobby was. She told them the candidate had won. "But how *is* he?" they insisted . . . and then, as realization dawned, broke the bad news. "It can't be," cried

Jacqueline Kennedy. Then, at 4:20 A.M. (E.D.T.) she telephoned *The New York Times* for whatever further information the newspaper might have.

Back in Los Angeles, the little man in blue had been searched, medically examined (he had sustained a broken index finger and a sprained ankle in the struggle following the shooting), photographed, and interrogated. He remained mute. Eyewitnesses to the shooting had described him as "Spanish-looking," "possibly a Filipino," "Mexican maybe," and "of Latin extraction." Police chief Thomas Reddin thought he might be a Cuban or a West Indian. He was five feet three inches tall, weighed 120 pounds, had brown eyes and thick black hair. He was entered on the police blotter as "John Doe," but was later identified as Sirhan Sirhan, the son of a Jordanian citizen, Bishara Sirhan.

Wednesday, June 5, dawned gray, and for the season, chilly, in Los Angeles. A red-eyed throng was waiting when Mankiewicz appeared, at 7:20 A.M. (Pacific time), dead-white in the glare of the television lights, to announce that the surgical team had finally completed its work, and that "all but one fragment of the bullet" had been removed from Kennedy's brain. The "next twelve to thirty-six hours," he added, would "be a very critical period." The news was not good, but thirty-six hours sounded, at least, like a future. Then the waiting and the silence continued excruciatingly until five-thirty that evening, when Mankiewicz moved to the microphones to say: "The team of physicians attending Senator Robert Kennedy is concerned over his continuing failure to show improvement during the postoperative period."

Mankiewicz did not reappear until one minute before two o'clock the following morning. "I have a short announcement to read," he said, "which I will read at this time." There was no need for him to read it. Anyone watching his face knew that Robert F. Kennedy—and an American dream—was dead.

Frank Mankiewicz, Kennedy's press secretary, an-nounced the senator's death on the morning of June 6.

The Last Thirty-six Hours

An eyewitness account by
Kristi N. Witker

*Kristi Witker covered Robert Kennedy's Indiana
and California campaigns for American Heritage,
and was with the senator at the time of the shooting.
Following are her recollections of the final day of
campaigning and of the fateful events of June 5.*

It would be the last day of campaigning before the
California primary. And it began just as all the
others had—a hurried breakfast, a frenzied dash for
the press bus, a drive to the airport, and then onto
the plane, which, strangely, although I had been on
only three Kennedy trips, had become my world. It
was 10:30 A.M. on a day that would take us from
Los Angeles to San Francisco, Long Beach, Venice, and San Diego before we returned at midnight.

We were all tired, but no one ever thought of
missing any part of a day's campaigning: there was
a unique cohesiveness about that group of aides,
reporters, and family friends traveling with Kennedy that is almost impossible to define to anyone
outside, but that, once you had experienced it,
pulled you back with an intense feeling of home-
sickness. On the plane, on the bus, at the hotel—
wherever—that group seemed to be the whole world
and there wasn't anything else that could measure
up to the sense of stimulation and well-being you
got when you were a part of it. No matter how
grueling the schedule, you didn't get tired when you
were following Kennedy from place to place because you were with the people you most wanted
to be with and doing the best thing you could be

doing. And then, though no one ever said it, there was the fear. I think all of us looked at crowds in a searching way—I found myself often gazing up at rooftops, at windows, at people's hands in the crowds, worrying and wondering, "Could it happen again?" Whenever the press bus fell behind the senator's car there was genuine consternation. Of course, the press always wants to be right with the candidate—but the cries of "catch up" were a little too shrill. It seemed much more than a desire to hear the first word of an already familiar speech.

From the San Francisco airport we drove to Chinatown, and in the crush of shouting humanity several of us were able to leap onto open cars for the motorcade. Hands were reaching for Bobby, pulling his hands and arms, and I said something about all the cuff links he had lost on the campaign. "Nixon's had the same pair of cuff links since 1945," Dick Drayne, one of Bobby's press secretaries, said, laughing. Then suddenly there was a sharp popping sound that made the words echo, and the street seemed to spin before me. Ethel had lurched and pulled Bobby down beside her. I thought, "It can't be . . . it can't be like this". . . and it wasn't. Someone said, "It's firecrackers." Ethel and Bobby sat up, and the street stopped spinning. The incident was cathartic. We'd gotten through it. The gods seemed to be saying, "See, everything's all right. It isn't going to happen."

On the plane trip to Long Beach we talked again about the television "debate" with Senator McCarthy two days earlier. Bobby had done well, most of us agreed, until the final question: he had looked startled when asked why he felt qualified to be President. I asked him what had happened, and he laughed. "Well," he said, "to tell you the truth, McCarthy was talking and I looked at the time clock and it said thirty and then fifteen, five, and zero. I thought it was over and I put the whole thing out of my mind. I was thinking where Ethel and I would have dinner when I suddenly heard 'You go first, Mr. Kennedy,'—and I hadn't heard the question."

The crowd in Long Beach was large and enthusiastic. But the rally ended on a sad note. As Kennedy left the makeshift podium, an unshaven, greasy-haired bystander began to scream, "Hey, Mr. Kennedy, who killed your brother?"

Under sunny skies, throngs of people cheered the motorcade through Long Beach, Watts, and Venice. But by the time we reached Santa Monica, a cold gray smog hung over the area, and at San Diego, to which we flew for the last rally of the California campaign, it was dark. It was just another reception except for one thing. Bob Kennedy got sick. He stopped speaking abruptly and sat down at the edge of the stage with his head in his hands. Rafer Johnson, Bill Barry, and Rosey Grier rushed up to him and led him off the stage—he had been seized with a stomach upset. But he returned for the second shift of listeners and was able to continue with his usual enthusiasm and humor. He ended without the all-too-familiar lines from Shaw —lines that had always made us groan, but that served as our signal to race for the press bus. Then, impishly, Bobby went on, to the bewilderment of his listeners and to the great delight of the press, "Oh, for the benefit of my friends on the left I want to add, as George Bernard Shaw once said, "Some men see things as they are and say why. I dream things that never were and say, why not.' "

That evening about twenty of us gathered in Kennedy's suite in the Ambassador Hotel (he was spending the night at John Frankenheimer's house in Malibu) and sang and danced until the early hours of morning. But beneath the gaiety was the thought that in one more day this whole wonderful group might be disbanded forever—all the plans, the hopes, the jokes, the talks, the daily schedules, the pleasure of spotting the Kennedy campaign badge on someone approaching in a hotel corridor. . . .

We had planned to have a party around the hotel pool on Tuesday—primary day—but the day dawned cool and overcast. Everyone got up late and scattered in different directions. Those who had stories to file had already done so. Now there was nothing to do but wait. TV crews were setting up in the Embassy Room on the Ambassador Hotel's main floor, campaign workers were hanging red, white, and blue streamers, and myriads of Kennedy posters, banners, and stickers suddenly seemed to engulf the hotel. I picked up my election-night press badge— it was bright blue and somehow very cheery looking. I thought what fun it would be in future years to have it as a souvenir—if Kennedy won. Everyone was telling me he would—Fred Dutton, Hugh McDonald, Dick Tuck—and pollster Oliver Quayle predicted a Kennedy victory by 9 percentage points. Then why didn't we all feel happier? We were all a little edgy after Oregon, we agreed, and it was such a gloomy day.

Later, I went up to Dick Drayne's room for a pre-election party, and then on to Senator Kennedy's suite on the fifth floor to watch the returns. It was 8:35 P.M. With 2 per cent of the vote in, the figures on the TV screen showed that McCarthy was ahead. A bar was set up in the corner of the living room, but few were drinking yet. Michael, David, Courtney, and Kerry Kennedy sat on the floor, all dressed in navy, sipping cokes and staring at TV. I asked Kerry whether she was enjoying the show and she giggled and spilled some coke—"It's fun and we can stay up late." More people were wandering up to the bar. All the familiar faces were there: Adam Walinsky, Jeff Greenfield, Theodore White, Jim Dunn, Bob Clark, Steve Smith, Loudon Wainwright, Stan Tretick of *Look,* Hays Gorey from *Time,* John Glenn and his wife and daughter, Jean Smith, and on and on. One network's computers projected a Kennedy victory by 48 per cent to 41 per cent. Dick Harwood and Pete Hamill came in, and then Frank Mankiewicz, who was smiling for what seemed to me the first time in days.

It was now 10:05 and another prediction gave him a 52 per cent lead to McCarthy's 38 per cent. A cheer went up in the room and suddenly Blanche Whittaker, a friend of Ethel's, was hugging everyone, and Adam and Jeff were grinning and drinking. McCarthy's face loomed on the screen and everyone crowded around to listen to him announce that he was "just beginning to fight." I walked into the hall just as Bobby stepped out of an adjacent room, alone for an instant. His face wore the usual quizzical expression, and I thought I should say something more than "congratulations." "What did you think of McCarthy just now?" I asked, and he answered quickly, "I'm not surprised—but I can only win with the help of those people [McCarthy's supporters]. It'll depend on how many put more faith in principle than in personality."

He turned to talk to his cousin Polly Fitzgerald, and crowds began to fill the hall. A boy in his early teens with a nasal voice was yelling, "Where's Senator Kennedy?" and when asked his purpose in being there, he began excitedly, "Jesse Unruh said I could come—it's a special favor, see—I'm doing this term paper and I've been working on it for three months. . . ." His voice trailed off and was replaced by a female one rasping out to a friend a detailed description of a magazine article about McCarthy.

Inside another room Bobby watched the returns with aides and reporters and planned his future. Later, the senator came out into the hall again, and we nearly collided. "I'm sorry, I'm really underfoot tonight," I apologized, and he laughed, and whispered, "We're having a party at The Factory afterwards—will you come?" I felt great. It was going to be a wonderful night. Marie Ritter of Ritter Publications was next to me. "I wish I could decide," she kept saying. "If I stay for the party, I'll miss the plane and tomorrow is my son's graduation. What shall I do? If I leave now, will I miss anything?" It was then 11:45.

It was getting very hot. A girl from CBS with a walkie-talkie stood nearby, saying into the microphone, "They're just about to leave the suite." Fred Dutton, Bill Barry, Jesse Unruh, and the Kennedys came out. I spotted the back of Rafer Johnson's head, and there was a crush of bodies as we all began to move down the fifth floor hall to the elevator. I wondered if all this heat and push were worth it—just to be up in front for the victory speech. I could probably see it much better on television back in the suite—but it was too late. The hall behind me was filled with people. I could only go forward.

And then we were on the stage in the glare of the TV lights and I saw that the Embassy Room was jammed. It was exhilarating—the infectious happiness, all the silly hats and banners. Somehow they were all good. They were part of a wonderful moment. I wondered if any TV stations in the East were still on, and I heard Bobby saying, "And I also want to thank, not necessarily in that order, my wife, Ethel," and the people were laughing. And then he was winding up—"I just got a call from Sam Yorty and he says we've been here long enough already. . . . So my thanks to all of you, and it's on to Chicago, and let's win!"

People were wildly applauding and cheering, and he and Ethel were turning to leave.

"We're going out the front," I thought. But then Bill Barry and Bobby were turning again and we were suddenly filing out through the back foyer and into the pantry. It was 12:15 A.M. I wondered if it would be too late to go to The Factory. I saw Bobby's head about six feet in front of me and scrambled to keep up. A young girl close by said, "Oh darn, he's always fooling us—he's taking the other way." And then there was a sudden sound of a balloon popping, and more balloons—or firecrackers—please, oh please, firecrackers. A man in front of me crumpled to his knees. His hair looked wet. There was a high-pitched scream. Another scream. Someone was running. A man was clutching his stomach. Near me someone was wailing, "Oh no, Oh no, Not again, Oh no." It was not a human sound. A voice, and then a chorus of voices, merged. "Get the gun, get the gun." The popping sound went on. There seemed to be at least eight gunmen. In back of me a voice cried, "This woman's been shot—help me." It didn't seem to matter. I couldn't move. I knew who the shots were for. There was nowhere to run to. Rafer, Bill Barry, and George Plimpton were wrestling with someone: there was only one gunman. And then Steve Smith's voice was calling in the distance, "Please clear the area. Please don't panic. Everything is all right." Maybe it was—it *had* to be all right. I looked down at Robert Kennedy, the man so brimming with life a second before, the man who had wanted to take his campaign "to the people" and who "refused to ride in an armored car," and for a second everything seemed the same. But then I saw his expression—it was not recognition, but resignation. Above the rising pitch of screams, I could hear someone cry, "Kill him—Kill him—Kill him now." A harsh voice sliced the air—"Get out of the way. I want this shot." And suddenly my legs were moving and I was backing away toward a table while a man focused his camera on Robert Kennedy. . . .

The looming TV cameras, shadowy lights, and clusters of reporters and bystanders gathering in front of Good Samaritan Hospital seemed as unreal and unbelievable as the sobbing Kennedy aides and praying campaign workers in the gaily decorated Ambassador Hotel lobby. From the first optimistic reports, Bobby's condition steadily worsened. It was almost impossible to reconcile the steely hospital and antiseptic operating room with the vital man we had known. They did not—could not—go together. Night turned into gray, chilly dawn. My radio told me it was 62 degrees. How odd that a day before, the weather had mattered.

At 7:20 A.M. Frank Mankiewicz announced that the operation was over and that Kennedy's condition was extremely critical. But we could not leave the hospital. Somehow it seemed if we all stayed together—that familiar group—everything might be the same again. And so the day passed and the night, and we talked and thought and cried and sometimes dared to hope. And then at 2:00 A.M. on Thursday morning, twenty-five hours and forty-four minutes after Senator Kennedy had left his tumultuous ovation in the Ambassador Hotel, Frank Mankiewicz entered the gymnasium that had served as our press room. "I have a short announcement to read, which I will read at this time," he said. "Senator Robert Francis Kennedy died at 1:44 A.M. today, June 6, 1968. . . . He was forty-two years old." The campaign was over.

Senator Kennedy's body was flown to New York on the evening of June 6, and was taken to St. Patrick's Cathedral, where one hundred thousand mourners paid their last respects to the fallen candidate. A funeral mass, at which Edward M. Kennedy eulogized his brother, was held on the morning of June 8. The casket was then placed aboard a train, which was scheduled to arrive in Washington around 5 P.M.; because of huge crowds all along the route the train did not reach the Capital until after nine o'clock. The cortege stopped briefly at the Justice Department, where Robert Kennedy had worked as Attorney General, and at the Lincoln Memorial, near Resurrection City, the temporary village established by members of the Poor People's Campaign. Then the body was borne to Arlington National Cemetery, where Robert Francis Kennedy was interred near the grave of his brother, the late President of the United States.

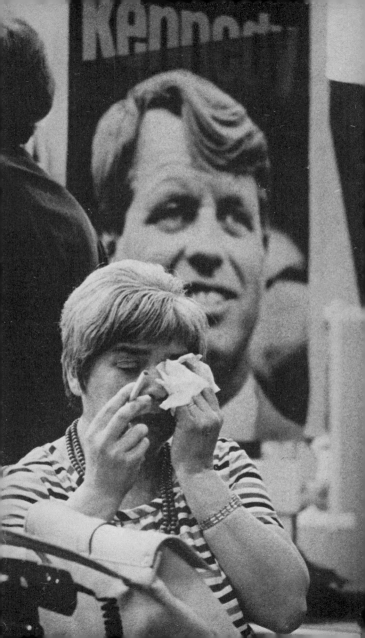

Picture Credits: